OCCASIONAL PAPERS IN INTERNATIONAL AFFAIRS
Number 26
NOVEMBER 1970

THE GERMAN DEMOCRATIC REPUBLIC
FROM THE SIXTIES TO THE SEVENTIES
A Socio-Political Analysis

By *Peter Christian Ludz*

with

FOREWORD

By

Professor Karl W. Deutsch

Published by the
Center for International Affairs
Harvard University

703544

ABOUT THE AUTHOR

Peter C. Ludz is Professor of Political Science at the University of Bielefeld in West Germany. He has taught at the Free University of Berlin and was, from 1968 to 1970, Visiting Professor and Senior Research Fellow at the Research Institute on Communist Affairs, Columbia University, New York City. Since 1967, Mr. Ludz has also been Consultant to the Ministry of All-German (now Intra-German) Affairs and to the Senate of Berlin.

His publications include: *Parteielite im Wandel* (Cologne-Opladen: Westdeutscher Verlag, 3rd printing, 1970, to appear in an American edition from M.I.T. Press in 1971); and, as editor, *Studien und Materialien zur Soziologie der DDR* (Cologne-Opladen: Westdeutscher Verlag, 1964), and two volumes of works by Georg Lukács, *Schriften zur Literatursoziologie* and *Schriften zur Ideologie und Politik* (Neuwied-Berlin: Luchterhand Verlag, 1961 and 1967).

Fuller knowledge of the Communist-ruled East German state —
the German Democratic Republic (GDR) — has long been
needed by anyone in the Western World who seeks a broader
understanding of the trends of world politics in the 1970s.

A study of the experiences of the GDR, of its mixture of con-
straint and growth, rigidities and change, can teach us many
things. It can tell us something about what a Communist regime
can or cannot do to a society: the potentialities and limits of Communist patterns of organization and ideology; the relation between
the new regime and existing local and national traditions, social
structures, and culture patterns; its handling of problems of economic growth and technological innovation, of science and mass
education; of the selection of cadres and elites, of the search for
mass support, and the socialization of the young. But it can also
tell us what a society and technology can do to a party and to its
ideology. The GDR did not rise spontaneously out of local political processes or out of any German revolution. Its basis was
created by the Soviet Army at the end of World War II. But
today, a quarter of a century later, the GDR is more than a mere
import. It has produced changes, and it has been changed itself.
If there has been a Communist impact on East Germany, there
has also been an East German impact on Communist practices
and institutions. The mutual interplay is likely to continue.

Another opportunity for better understanding comes from comparison. How are some of the problems of modern industrial
societies dealt with in the GDR, in comparison to their treatment
in the German Federal Republic, in the U.S.S.R., and in the
United States? Everywhere, advanced industrialization creates
problems of mass mobilization and elite selection, of claims for
more leisure, higher living standards and more varied life styles,

together with greater needs for high performance, for dependable self-motivation and reliability, and for creative innovation and initiatives. These matters clash, at least in part. How are their tensions and conflicts managed in Eastern Germany, in comparison to experience in the GFR, the U.S.S.R., and the United States? We have come to the point where we can treat the social system itself as a variable, and try to find out how much or how little difference it makes.

Professor Peter Christian Ludz is one of the leading experts in the Western world on the GDR. His pioneering book on its ruling party, *A Party Elite in Transformation (Parteielite im Wandel)* is quickly becoming a classic. But Professor Ludz is not merely an area specialist. He is a political theorist and a comparative student with broad interests, with much to say on many aspects of modern politics. This brief publication bears the mark of a powerful mind for whom political science is one way to discovery about how people share in the making of their fate.

By the same token, this short work cannot deal with all the questions it raises. But it does raise many of the right questions, and it is full of relevant information. In deepening our knowledge, in raising questions of basic insight and of current policy, in exposing his views to scholarly criticism, and in demonstrating objectivity without indifference, Professor Ludz has made a contribution to the program of our Center.

KARL W. DEUTSCH
*Faculty Associate
of the Center*

PREFACE

This study is a revised version of a series of lectures given by the author in October 1968, at a seminar of the German Research Program, organized and directed by Professor Henry A. Kissinger at Harvard University. Although the GDR image has changed since 1968, these lectures may still present a meaningful framework within which the GDR may with profit be studied. The politics of a state cannot be properly analyzed without adequate consideration of its social composition, the behavior of social groups, or the role of its social norms. Also, politics must be analyzed with reference to the economic conditions of a country. It is the consideration of such fundamental socio-economic factors that gives meaning to political analysis.

The author wishes to thank all those who have made these lectures and their publication possible. In particular the author is grateful to Professor Henry A. Kissinger of Harvard University for his invitation to present these lectures. Dr. Guido Goldman, also of Harvard, provided helpful suggestions and support. The author gained many insights in the discussions of the seminar, especially from Professors Carl Joachim Friedrich and Karl W. Deutsch of Harvard and from Professor William E. Griffith of the Massachusetts Institute of Technology, to all of whom he would like to express his appreciation.

The author is grateful also to the Research Institute on Communist Affairs of Columbia University and especially to its director, Professor Zbigniew Brzezinski, for making possible the revision of this manuscript for publication. He is especially indebted to Edward L. McGowan of the Research Institute on Communist Affairs, who collaborated with the author in the translation of the text.

PETER C. LUDZ

TABLE OF CONTENTS

LIST OF TABLES

List of Abbreviations

CDU	Christlich-Demokratische Union (Christian Democratic Union)
COMECON	Council for Mutual Economic Aid
DBD	Demokratische Bauernpartei Deutschlands (German Democratic Farmers' Party)
FDGB	Freier Deutscher Gewerkschaftsbund (Free German Trade Union Federation)
FDJ	Freie Deutsche Jugend (Free German Youth)
KPD	Kommunistische Partei Deutschlands (German Communist Party)
LDPD	Liberal-Demokratische Partei Deutschlands (German Liberal Democratic Party)
LPG	Landwirtschaftliche Produktionsgenossenschaften (Agricultural Production Co-ops)
NDPD	National-Demokratische Partei Deutschlands (National Democratic Party of Germany)
NVA	Nationale Volksarmee (National People's Army)
SED	Sozialistische Einheitspartei Deutschlands (Socialist Unity Party)
SPD	Sozialdemokratische Partei Deutschlands (Social Democratic Party)
VVB	Vereinigungen Volkseigener Betriebe (Association of State-Owned Enterprises)

INTRODUCTION

With the Warsaw Pact occupation of Czechoslovakia in August 1968, East Germany once again became a topic of live interest to the world press. This is not surprising, because the invasion marked the second time within thirty years that German troops had occupied or at least "co-occupied" that country. Furthermore, in the summer and fall of 1968, many political observers feared that the occupation of Czechoslovakia was to be only the first in a series of repressive Soviet moves and that the next political or military step by the Soviet Union, and the German Democratic Republic, would be directed against West Berlin. By the spring of 1969, however, when the presidential elections of the Federal Republic of Germany were held in West Berlin without undue commotion, it became clear that these fears had been unfounded. Evidently, in the case of Czechoslovakia, the Soviet Union had acted more out of intra-bloc considerations than out of aggressive intentions toward the West.

Nevertheless, this "rediscovery," so to speak, of East Germany gave rise to a whole series of questions, especially in the United States. They ranged from speculations about Ulbricht's role in the occupation of Czechoslovakia to the question of the degree to which the GDR had actually been integrated into Eastern Europe. Was the Eastern bloc still the same satellite system it had been in Stalin's time? Had the domestic situation in the GDR changed fundamentally since the construction of the Berlin Wall in August 1961?

With the advantage of hindsight, it is relatively clear that in the summer of 1968 Ulbricht's influence had been considerable. His aim in using it — and in this he was successful — was to prove himself a reliable partner to the Soviet leaders in a crisis situation. In addition, the role played by the GDR in the events of 1968 forced even those who still thought of it as a Stalinist appendage of the USSR to take note of Ulbricht's growing influence, of the GDR's expanded economic and political role in COMECON, and of its activities in the Near East, Africa, and South America.

[1]

A broader question — whether the German Democratic Republic had developed from a Soviet Occupation Zone (SOZ) into an authentic and new "second Germany," possessing its own political climate — is much more difficult to assess. A first glance shows a society with many contradictory features. Tendencies toward social pluralism exist in a one-party state. Authoritarian-technocratic controls of force, terror, and suppression, exercised by the bureaucracy, have become more and more pronounced. On the other hand, the society appears to have a high degree of social mobility and dynamism and, compared with the Federal Republic, to show unusual features of modernization. Thus the traditional, or communist, power structures exist among tendencies toward modernization. The simultaneous existence of these contradictory and shifting patterns makes the deeper study of contemporary East Germany particularly challenging.

Various empty normative concepts such as "totalitarianism" and "re-Stalinization," which have often been used to describe the GDR, now seem to say very little. But new schematizations on the order of "liberalization" should also be avoided. When subjected to rigorous historical testing and methodological critique these abstract normative formulas have proven of minimal analytical use. Since the end of the Stalinist period it has become abundantly clear that certain *a priori* assumptions about the essential nature of "totalitarian dictatorship" were inadequate to explain the dynamics of communist systems. This holds in particular for the thesis that national socialism and Soviet communism are "basically alike." This has proven more a hindrance than a help in the analysis of communist systems.

Therefore, in order to gauge the social dynamics and political possibilities of East German society more accurately, it would appear more meaningful to undertake a close socio-political analysis of certain fundamental aspects of its domestic and foreign policy. Instead of dealing primarily with methodological problems of East European research, the following pages will describe and examine some of the politically relevant factors of social structure and political and social change in East Germany.

Some Background Data

The GDR covers an area of 41,659 square miles, or about 23 per cent of the area of the German *Reich* of 1937. On the north, the GDR is bordered by the Baltic Sea; on the south, by Czechoslovakia; on the west, by the Federal Republic. On the east, the Oder and Neisse rivers form the boundary with Poland.

When a part of the German *Reich*, the present GDR was an area with an agricultural surplus; today it is noted rather for its industrial production. With the exception of sugar and eggs, foodstuffs are for the most part imported. The main natural resources include copper (Ostharz), uranium (Erzgebirge), and lignite (Leipzig and Lower Lusatia). Eight industrial regions can be identified: the Magdeburg-Harz area (mainly heavy and light industry); the Halle-Leipzig area (mainly coal mining and chemical industry); the Erfurt-Gera area (mainly light industry and automobile manufacturing); the Karl-Marx-Stadt area (mainly textiles); the Dresden area (electro-technical and mechanical industry, textiles, and food industry); the Cottbus-Lusatia area (lignite mining and processing); the area around Berlin (electro-technical and mechanical industry), including Frankfurt-on-the-Oder (steel production, petroleum products) and Brandenburg (agricultural machinery industry); and the Rostock area (ship-building industry).[1]

Since 1952 the GDR has been divided into fifteen administrative districts called *Bezirke*: Berlin (East), Cottbus, Dresden, Erfurt, Frankfurt, Gera, Halle, Karl-Marx-Stadt, Leipzig, Magdeburg, Neubrandenburg, Potsdam, Rostock, Schwerin and Suhl. The three largest *Bezirke* (Potsdam, Magdeburg, Neubrandenburg) are primarily agricultural. The *Bezirke* consist of 26 *Stadtkreise,* or urban districts, and 191 *Landkreise*, or rural districts. The smallest administrative units are *Gemeinden*, or local communes, which total 9,011.

In 1946 approximately 18.5 million people lived in what is now the GDR. At the end of 1968, the population came to only about 17.1 million, of whom barely 1.1 million lived in East Berlin. From 1946 to 1961 about 0.5 per cent of the population had fled from the GDR every year.[2] Of the 1968 population of 17.1 million, about 7.8 million were males and about 9.3 million females. The age structure is probably the most unfavorable in all of Europe. The birth rate is relatively low (1968: 14.3 live births per 1,000 people), and it has been falling steadily since 1963. In contrast, the mortality rate is relatively high: in 1967 there were 227,068 deaths (i.e., 13.3 per 1,000 people) for 252,817 live births.[3] In 1968, the groups of working age (15 to 65, or 15 to 60 in the case of women) came to 9.88 million, of whom 4.83

[3]

million were males and 5.05 million were females. Of this total potential work force, 7.71 million, or about 78 per cent, were actually employed, of them 3.66 million being females. Of the total actual working force of 7.71 million, 2.82 million were employed in industry and 1.07 million in agriculture. Trade took 880,000; transportation and communication, 540,000; construction, 520,000; and handicrafts, 400,000. The remaining 1.48 million were scattered throughout other areas.[4]

Three Stages of Development: 1945–1969

A retrospective view makes it possible to identify roughly three stages of development in the SOZ/GDR since 1945.

The first stage: 1945–1952. These years were used by the German Communist Party (KPD) and the Soviets and, after 1946, increasingly by the Socialist Unity Party (SED) to destroy the remnants of the political and social structure of the old German *Reich*. Particularly significant in this regard were the nationalization of key industries, the abolition, as early as the summer of 1945, of the professional civil service (*Berufsbeamtentum*), and the so-called Land Reform of 1945–1946, which actually meant state confiscation of all agricultural enterprises of over 100 hectares. In addition, the collapse of 1945 led to the radical reorganization of political life. Thus, the SED absorbed the (East) German Social Democratic Party (SPD) after their unification in April 1946 and the bourgeois parties — the Christian Democratic Union (CDU, founded in 1945), and the German Liberal Democratic Party (LDPD, also founded in 1945) — were transformed into satellite parties. In 1948 the German National Democratic Party (NDPD) and the German Democratic Farmers' Party (DBD) were established: the function of the first was to integrate former officers and the bourgeois middle class into political life, the function of the second was to do the same thing with the farmers. And in 1950, a united trade union, the Free German Trade Union Confederation (FDGB), was founded. Finally, in 1952, the five existing *Laender* (Brandenburg, Mecklenburg, Saxony, Saxe-Anhalt, Thuringia) were replaced by the fifteen smaller administrative units called *Bezirke*. The central administrative bodies were thus strengthened considerably.

The GDR was proclaimed an independent German state in October 1949, about a month after the founding of the Federal

Republic of Germany. Ratification of the first East German Constitution took place on October 7, 1949, in the *Deutscher Volksrat*, which at the same time also declared itself to be a "provisional People's Chamber" (*provisorische Volkskammer*). The 1949 Constitution reaffirmed the principle of "people's sovereignty" as fundamental and listed a wide range of individual civil rights.

In its terms this Constitution was quite close to that of the 1919 Weimar Republic, since it also contained elements of federation and reiterated the principle of the rule of law. At that time the SED obviously hoped that this Constitution could become the charter for a united Germany. For this reason the 1949 document emphasized a "single" German citizenship. Only in the 1967 Statute of Citizenship was GDR citizenship unequivocally proclaimed.

In 1950 the GDR was incorporated into COMECON. It is clear from directives issued under the First Five Year Plan, which began in 1951, that the GDR's economy was already primarily oriented toward the needs of the Soviet Union.

The second stage: 1952–1961. Especially in the official historiography of the GDR, 1952 has been viewed as a most significant year. It was in July of that year, at the Second Conference of the SED, that the "construction of socialism," to take place over the next ten years, was proclaimed. As a result of various accompanying changes, Walter Ulbricht in 1953 moved from his post of General Secretary to that of First Secretary of the SED Central Committee and proceeded to press ahead relentlessly. By February 1958 he had solidified his position of power by eliminating the party opposition, particularly his most important rivals, Wilhelm Zaisser and Karl Schirdewan.[4a]

In general, this stage was characterized by the so-called "class struggle within" and by a continuous reorganization in almost all areas of party, state, economy, and society. Not only did the SED leadership systematically try to place its loyal cadres in all these areas; it also methodically destroyed the remnants of private property and of the older social structure in commerce, the small crafts and trades, agriculture, and industry. In order to accomplish these purposes, the SED established "production co-operatives" in the first three of these fields. As for individual businesses,

[5]

their management, control, and organization were transferred to collective entities controlled by the SED.

Agriculture bore the brunt of this interference, with force being used to remodel the organization of production under the leadership of party cadres. Thus, in the spring of 1960, all remaining independent farmers were forced to join Agricultural Production Co-ops (*Landswirtschaftliche Produktionsgenossenschaften*, or LPGs). At that time there were about 19,000 LPGs of different degrees of socialization.[5] Since they have been gradually consolidated, the number of LPGs has steadily decreased. In 1968 there were only 11,513, with some 960,000 members.

From the beginning, the SED party leadership combined the destruction of traditional organizational forms and other parts of the inherited social structure with the will to develop the GDR into a strong industrial state. This state was to be a potential and reliable junior partner of the Soviet Union, as independent as possible from the West, in particular from West Germany. This goal was pursued both by Soviet leaders, who recognized the GDR as a sovereign state in 1955, and by Ulbricht and those members of the SED Politburo who were faithful to him.

On the whole, however, the political, economic, and, in particular, the psychological achievements of the SED in these years were relatively limited. Numerous factors were responsible for this: the unfavorable postwar economic situation; the reparations due the USSR (through 1954); the impractical overbureaucratization; the unsuccessful beginnings of educational reform; the intra-party struggles; and the continuing political emigration to the West, especially of people of working age.

The third stage: 1961 to 1969. This stage begins with the construction of the Berlin Wall on August 13, 1961, that is, with the artificial self-isolation of the GDR. In a more specific sense this stage began early in 1963, at the Sixth Party Congress of the SED, when, in connection with Khrushchev's reforms of the fall of 1962, Ulbricht announced an extensive modernization of the entire system.

The nucleus of his program was the "new economic system of planning and management of the people's economy."[6] As is customary at communist party congresses, Ulbricht criticized the deficiencies of the economy. In addition, he for the first time outlined a relatively realistic picture of the socio-economic situation

[6]

of the GDR. He was helped to do so by a favorable domestic and international situation. For one thing, the construction of the Wall had halted the mass exodus of fugitives to the West. For another, business, industry, and agriculture had begun to recover from the severe set-backs of 1958–1962. Finally, Ulbricht possessed the full backing of the Soviets.

Compared to the unrealistic goal expressed in 1958, which had been to catch up to or even to surpass the Federal Republic in per capita consumption within several years, the economic goals of 1963 were far more carefully formulated. The concepts of profit, cost, price, profit-earning capacity, economic cost-accounting were finally accepted as principles of industrial management in the GDR. Wages and bonuses were raised, and therefore the situation of the working population was considerably improved. Even more important was the, at first hesitant, recognition of the principle of performance (*Leistungsprinzip*). Already codified in the Labor Code (*Gesetzbuch der Arbeit*) of 1961, the *Leistungsprinzip* meant that wages in industry etc. were to be set according to the workers' performance. Those who did better work were to be paid higher salaries. Thus individuals and groups were mobilized via their so-called "material interest." In addition to improving the training system, such mobilization had the positive effect of increasing efficiency in business and industry. The effectiveness of the principle of performance was not, however, confined to business life. In one way or another, from 1961 on, it put its stamp upon East German history in general.

The program for the "new economic system" also included plans for greater industrial decentralization, a rationalization of the bureaucracy throughout the entire economy, and a greater flexibility in decision-making in enterprises. Such plans were especially relevant to the key industries: the chemical industry, the electro-technical and electronic industry, and the optical machine-building industry.

With the announcement of this reform program, the earlier policies of compulsory nationalization – i.e., the transfer of private property to collective state ownership – could be considered as good as completed. In 1963 socialized industry contributed 85.5 per cent of the gross national product; in 1967, 86.8 per cent. While in 1963 the so-called semi-state companies – i.e., those operating with state participation – produced 6.7 per cent of the gross national product, in 1967 they produced 7.2 per cent. In

[7]

these five years the contribution of private enterprise decreased by almost 25 per cent: to 6.0 per cent in 1967 as compared with 7.8 per cent in 1963.[7]

Parallel to these measures in the area of economics were radical changes in party and state structure. The most important reform was the introduction of what might be called "staffs" at all levels of the state and party bureaucracies.[8] These staffs had more than a consultative function; they were also to transform party resolutions into economic and social reality. This process now took place much less bureaucratically and much more pragmatically than it had in the fifties — partly because the staffs were composed of younger specialists who were less dependent on the traditional dogmatic ideology.

Finally, during this period, the SED leadership wanted to try to win the support of the people, whose attitude had always ranged from suspicion to hostility. It therefore struck a more conciliatory tone and made many small concessions affecting day-to-day life. However, the party's cultural and religious policies remained untouched by these developments, and in these fields the hard line of the fifties changed very little.

To sum up, since 1963 the SED leadership has not been concerned merely with safeguarding its power. It has also aimed at a functioning economic and social order in the GDR. In so doing, it has to an unprecedented extent accepted the development of economic and social forces independent of party controls. Naturally, a series of new conflicts has cropped up, for the rules deduced from the principles of performance and industrial efficiency often called for decisions that were incompatible with the needs of a centrally planned economy of the communist type.

The Methodological Approach

In the third stage of development, from 1961 to 1969, evidence of comprehensive social change and modernization appeared for the first time since the war. Some of this evidence will be discussed below, first, in terms of its political relevance; second, in relation to the historical background, i.e., the development of the GDR over the last twenty-five years; and, finally, in comparison with certain corresponding tendencies in the Federal Republic.

For such an analysis, examination of the constitutions of the GDR (1949, 1968), of the various SED statutes (1946, 1950,

[8]

1954, 1963), and of the 1963 program of the SED can only yield a superficial frame of reference.[9] A glance at the new Constitution shows clearly the changes that have taken place since 1949. In its 1949 Constitution, for example, the GDR was "a democratic republic;" it is now "a socialist state of German nation." Besides, in this definition and in some of its other clauses confirming the division of Germany (see Preamble and Article 8), the new Constitution, in contrast to the 1949 Constitution, explicitly stresses the unique role of the SED leadership. Article 1 of the new Constitution begins as follows: "The German Democratic Republic is a socialist state of German nation. It is the political organization of the working people in town and countryside who are jointly implementing socialism under the leadership of the working class and its Marxist-Leninist party." [10]

One-party leadership is not the only factor to characterize the GDR as a non-democratic social and political order. Some basic rights which have appeared in democratic constitutions are also lacking. For example, one looks in vain for the right to strike, the freedom to dissent, the right to emigrate, to free choice of profession, and to freedom in scientific research and teaching. Furthermore, basic "rights" of the citizens are supplemented by basic "duties." In addition, the basic rights are to be exercised and performed "in accordance with the spirit and aims" of the Constitution. Freedom of assembly, for example, exists only "within the framework of the principles and aims of the Constitution" (Article 28). Regulations (*Bestimmungen*) concerning freedom of opinion (Article 27) and association (Article 29) are similar. A number of additional restrictions can be cited. For example, the autonomy of religious denominations is no longer constitutionally guaranteed (compare Article 39 of the 1968 Constitution with Articles 41–44 of the 1949 Constitution). On the other hand, the "basic social rights" of the citizens are covered relatively extensively. The "right to leisure time and recreation" (Article 34) is guaranteed, as is the "right to social care in case of old age and invalidity" (Article 36). Health protection is provided (Article 35) and "marriage, family and motherhood" are placed "under the special protection of the state" (Article 38).

Although these clauses clearly characterize the GDR as a non-democratic or "totalitarian" state, they should not lead the analyst to premature normative evaluations. Because of its clear-cut and often highly moralized distinction between democratic and non-democratic systems of rule, a constitutional approach would, in this context, obscure a clear view of GDR society instead of leading to its realistic interpretation.

Sole reliance on constitutional interpretation would leave many basic questions unanswered: what, for example, are the goals of the constitutionally established party in domestic and foreign policy? How have its goals and methods changed over the years? How do citizens adjust to a system of constitutionally restricted rights? What are the people's reactions to the SED's policies? How is the fact that the GDR is now an industrial society — with numerous signs of the differentiation and social pluralism that can also be seen in Western industrial societies — to be evaluated?

Any precise description of the socio-political changes and the general lines of development in East German society is limited by the present research situation. Our knowledge of the second German state and society is unquestionably much more detailed and more comprehensive today than it was even a few years ago. But since for the most part we have to rely on East German sources, our picture remains incomplete. As a result, we must restrain ourselves from too many categorial statements about this society and from attempting to project a complete picture of it.

Therefore, in the social sphere we shall spotlight only some selected developments. These particular trends have been chosen for two reasons: 1) they do in fact represent major aspects of post–1961 change in the GDR; 2) in addition, enough data to document these particular processes of change are available. However, in order not to distort the findings drawn from available materials, we have refrained from applying sophisticated methodologies and have limited ourselves to a descriptive analysis of some major trends of change.

SOME OBSERVATIONS ON SOCIAL
AND POLITICAL CHANGE IN THE GDR

New Relations between the Party and the Population

The process of social and political change in the GDR first became apparent in the fifties. Becoming even more obvious since August 13, 1961, it was strengthened further after the Sixth and Seventh Party Congresses of the SED, held in January 1963 and April 1967, respectively. The social and political changes in question can be traced to several conspicuous causes. First and foremost, there was the construction of the Wall in August 1961. The resulting halt in the exodus to the West forced many of the groups within the population to "integrate" themselves into the social, though not necessarily into the political, process. Numerous groups, especially the party itself and the workers, were thus compelled to make more allowances for each other than heretofore. This process of "adaptation" was expressed in many ways. A partial adjustment of the SED to the population at large was, for example, evidenced by the fact that it came to be quite enough if the average man was competent and successful in professional life. He no longer also had to express his reliability in terms of the shibboleths of allegiance to the party and to the "first German worker-and-peasant state" and he no longer had to take part in public demonstrations and all types of mass organizational activities under the control of the SED. It was true that the professionally ambitious man who aspired to a leading position in business and society had to be a member of the SED. But party membership *per se* was often accepted as sufficient proof of party allegiance. For their part, many of the people no longer saw in every party measure some form of terroristic coercion or of deception.

This mutual adaptation led to a partial identity of interest between party and people. In 1963, at the Sixth Party Congress of the SED, Ulbricht emphasized that one sign of a developed

[11]

industrial society was a high standard of living. As a result of this announcement, the masses of working people began to feel that, at least in this area, their aspirations if not their motives conformed to those of the SED. In respect to the standard of living, the people tended to compare their situation with the situation in West Germany, where the standard was some 30 per cent higher than in the GDR. For its part, the SED leadership saw to it that the GDR standard of living surpassed that of the Soviet Union and other East European countries by at least 30 per cent. They justified their call for a constant increase in productivity by pointing to the gradual improvement in the standard of living. These facts must be seen in relation to the very impressive "boot strap" effort made to build up the GDR economy. As the positive results gradually became more and more apparent, especially in modern building construction, a greater "national" self-consciousness and a pride in achievement also grew, especially since the circumstances were more difficult than in the Federal Republic. The slogan, "Economic Miracle GDR," was a clever SED propaganda device but it found a response among thousands of people.

Thirdly, since 1963 changes could be seen in the SED's methods of government. In the forties and fifties, the major social and political objectives of the SED leadership had often been achieved through mass terror. Ideological and political in their motivation (as in Russia during the twenties and thirties), these terror tactics were directed against entire social classes. In the GDR the farmers, the middle classes, and the upper-middle and upper class (*Grossbourgeoisie*) were in particular subject to this terror over a period of many years. The linking of terror with a dogmatic, rigid, ideological system is frequently taken to be the major characteristic of totalitarian rule in general, as, for example, in the theories of Hannah Arendt and Carl Joachim Friedrich.[11] Since 1963, however, a broad selection of compulsory measures has taken the place of mass terror. These measures include a "selective" terror directed against specific individuals and small groups, but no longer against large groups and entire social classes. The theme of the "class struggle within" has been muted. This is evident, for example, in recent compulsory socializing of property in industry, crafts, trade, and ancillary industries, which is being carried on on an individual basis.

In addition to this form of terror, mention should be made

[12]

of an expanded system of institutionalized social controls, seen for example in the Youth Law (*Jugendgesetz*, 1964), the Family Law (*Familiengesetz*, 1965), and the Education Law (*Bildungsgesetz*, 1966). These legal codes contain definite regulations and social norms which are binding on the individual citizen. The effectiveness of these control measures is strengthened by the fact that certain principles of the social and value order in the GDR have become accepted as established in practice. This holds true for the people as well as for the SED. Therefore, more often than before, the party leadership foregoes tracing the genealogy of each measure adopted back to the basic revolutionary principles of marxism-leninism. It has, in other words, adapted its ideological dogma to actual social and economic developments. After twenty-five years, many everyday expressions in the official language, and certain standards and sanctions, have become more "internalized" by the people. One accepts them or circumvents them silently — which is in effect a form of acceptance. Such developments indicate that GDR society is being increasingly transformed into an authoritarian system. Totalitarian facets of rule are gradually receding into the background.

And finally, the attitude of the younger generation may be added to the above listing. The generation conflict manifests itself differently in the GDR than it does for example in the Federal Republic. In the FRG the protest of the younger generation often displays anarchistic strains and a tendency to question the whole social order. In the GDR, generational conflict has been confined by the party. The rising adult generation is basically not hostile toward the existing social order. It would, however, like to create a modern socialist system, which could react to challenges in a "creatively" more flexible manner.

Rationalization of the Economy and Some Implications

The rationalization of the economic system, which has so far been successful, is not only being intensified but its basic principles are also being extended to other areas of society, especially to the scientific and educational spheres.

As has already been pointed out, in 1963 the GDR had entered upon a "new economic system" — to which many observers had attached the futile hope of a political liberalization. The first stage of this new system was in 1967 superseded by a second

[13]

stage, called the "economic system of socialism." [12] Evidently it had at some point become clear that the central problems of a planned economy — problems involving information, management, and control — could not be solved by the mere introduction of a "new economic system."

This second stage is programmed to continue until 1975 and is apparently to adhere to the basic features of the "new economic system." Among these basic features are: recognition of the performance principle, the use of economic cost-accounting, profit, and earning power as principles of economic management, and the maintenance of a certain autonomy for corporations, large enterprises, and the regional economic bureaucracies. The responsibilities of export firms in decision-making have also steadily been expanded.

It is clear from the above that central planning and supervision have been reaffirmed in importance throughout the entire political and social system. However, in the new stage, centralized planning is on the whole supposed to be more flexibly organized. This is made particularly clear by the very high priority placed on the principle that decisions should be made wherever they can be most expertly made.

For the next few years the main problem facing the GDR's economy will be the attainment of a sufficiently high rate of economic growth. Extensive growth faces definite limitations, since the two basic growth factors, i.e., size of the work force and basic industrial capacity, are more apt to remain constant than to increase, at least until 1975. For this reason, opportunities for expansion lie chiefly in scientific and technological modernization. The imposing economic successes which had by 1967 brought the GDR up to eighth place in world industrial production and had seen industrial production increase by 471 per cent between 1950 and 1968, could hardly be expected to continue on the same scale. [13] The annual average growth rate of 6.0 per cent, which was projected for 1969 and subsequently, seems attainable only if the productivity of the entire industrial system actually rises at a projected average annual rate of 9.0 per cent, which is, practically speaking, a very dim possibility. In selected intensive growth industries, as in certain branches of the machine-building industry (the automobile and ship machinery industry), the rate of productivity is scheduled to rise by 10 per cent; in the electro-technical and electronic industry, by 11 per cent;

[14]

and in the chemical industry, by 12 per cent. These basic branches of the national economy will thus have to support the expansion of the GDR's exports, which is a *sine qua non* for future economic development. (There was a planned increase in exports of 10 per cent for 1969 and 12 per cent for 1970.)

The projected rates of increase in the most important branches of industry would seem to be realistic, *provided* certain conditions are met. One such condition is that the SED, the State Planning Commission, and the ministries of industry be able to solve the manifold information and communication problems within the society and the economy. In this connection, the improvement of partially obsolete communication and informa tion systems (postal and telecommunication systems) should be singled out for attention. A further condition is that investments planned for the capital construction industry be fully implemented. And, if only for psychological reasons, a final condition for speedy economic growth would be that the present property structure of private industry be maintained.

Since, for the above reasons, an extensive economic expansion can hardly be possible until at best 1975, the immediate economic growth of the GDR is dependent on the possibility of an "intensive" type of expansion. *The* prerequisite for this type of expansion is the swift and efficient reorganization of existing capacities for research and training. The qualitative improvement of scientific equipment, e.g., the computer industry, is just as urgent. In the last few years several electronic analog and digital computers have been developed. They are being exported in increasing numbers to the Soviet Union, Poland, and Czechoslovakia.

However, since 1967, priority has been given not only to a discussion of technological development and of the automatization and standardization of production procedure, but also to the reorganization of higher educational facilities. The purpose of such reorganization would be to tie scientific research and learning in the universities and technical and other colleges (*Hochschulen*) and the higher technical schools (*Fachhochschulen*) more closely to the production industries themselves. For example, the long-standing contractual relations between the Technical University of Dresden, the Bergakademie Freiberg, and several higher technical schools, on the one hand, and the chemical and electro-technical industries and concerns which manu-

[15]

facture machine tools and processing machinery on the other are to be extended to all scientific areas.

In terms of organization, this effort has led to far-reaching changes in the traditional structures of learning, though, in spite of all interference, they still continue to exist. It has also led to the incorporation of the institutions of learning into, or their affiliation with, existing Associations of State-Owned Enterprises (*Vereinigungen Volkseigener Betriebe*, or VVBs), Scientific-Technical Centers (*Wissenschaftliche-Technische Zentren*, or WTZ), and Industrial Institutes.

The long-term goal of the regime is the eventual formation of large-scale research organizations (*Grossforschungsverbände*) or scientific corporations (*wissenschaftliche Kombinate*). For this reorganization of the universities and technical colleges, the regime is taking as its point of departure the principle of the "section," which can be compared to the principle of the American university department. With time, even the most important mass organizations in science and technology — URANIA and the Chamber of Technology (*Kammer der Technik*, or KdT) — are to be incorporated into the contemplated large research organizations. At some future date, therefore, these large-scale research organizations will be just as dominant in the scientific and technological fields as the "socialist trusts" now are in industry. Electronic data-processing, modern cost-accounting methods, efficiency-evaluation techniques in the enterprises, and similar innovations will in the future be applied to the operations of scientific institutions as well.

There has also been change in the nature of scientific research itself. The regime has often stated its intention to see to the direct and expeditious application of scientific knowledge to industrial production and to the expansion and improvement of mass production, primarily for the East European markets. As a result, scientific research is increasingly being channelled into applied research for the benefit of the State-Owned Enterprises. The goal is therefore not so much to obtain new results from research and to use them in production, but to use existing knowledge as effectively and as quickly as possible to enhance mass production techniques and therefore commercial success. Since the total research capacity is limited, basic research has decreased.

Furthermore, in order to meet the problems of an expanding export industry, the applied research has itself had to become

[16]

more specialized. Since elsewhere the general trend of scientific research is toward both specialization and massive basic research (as for example in the United States), this limiting policy may in the next few years bring serious economic consequences for the GDR. Later, it may have serious political consequences as well. This conscious emphasis on the markets of today is at the expense of the markets of tomorrow. A short-range economic expansion achieved through intensification of applied research may be followed by a considerable economic contraction after 1975. By then, at the latest, this "overconcentration" on certain selected branches of research will certainly begin to take its toll. So will the dearth of basic pure research, should it be allowed to continue.

We cannot today predict the full *political* ramifications of such developments. However, one possible consequence might be a decline in the international prestige of the GDR. We may be sure however that the SED leadership is well aware of this potential danger and that it is trying to strengthen the international stature of the GDR as much and as quickly as possible.

This reorganization of science and research has been accompanied by a new conception of education on the university and college levels. It is now thought that such education should be primarily research-oriented, with research and theory both seeking to advance performance. In view of this orientation toward research as well as of the general reorganization in the scientific field, educational planners in the GDR hope to achieve greater "efficiency" in higher learning through the "speed-up" of courses and the "maximization" of education's practical impact on the economy. Along with the reorganization of full-time study (*Direktstudium*), the formerly scattered responsibility for refresher courses (*Weiterbildung*) has once more been allocated to the universities. In the future, *Weiterbildung* is to be considered as important as basic academic training. With the help of various new educational regulations, it is hoped by 1980 to increase by 250 per cent the number of persons with scientific training working in the economy. It is also hoped by the same time to increase the number of scientists and technicians by 350 per cent, using 1967 as the starting point.[14] It is clear that those who enter professional life from 1985 on will have to meet professional demands and standards which do not even exist today.

[17]

The Population and Occupation Structures

Because of the exodus of refugees, the population structure as well as the labor force and occupational structures have changed considerably. The effects of the mass flight of refugees to West Germany will be felt for a long time. It has been calculated that, at the least, some 2 to 2.5 million people — 15 per cent of the population of working age in 1950 — left the GDR from 1950 to 1963.[15]

An immediate consequence of the flight of millions of people from the GDR was the superannuation of the population. This came about because groups between 16 and 65 (or for women 60) years of age were overrepresented among the refugees: 77 per cent of all refugees were in these age groups, which comprised only 63 per cent of the population. Of the approximately 17.1 million people living in the GDR at the end of 1968, about 57.8 per cent were of working age and 19.3 per cent of retirement age. Children under 15 years of age made up 22.9 per cent of the total. In 1968, for every 100 people of working age there were 73 who were not yet (or no longer) able to work. In 1961, this figure had been only 65.9 and in 1950 only 56.1 for every 100.[16] According to available forecasts, the working-age population will in relative terms diminish even more in the next few years, so that in 1970 about 75 people who are not yet working or no longer able to work will have to be supported by every 100 workers. The labor force will level off until 1975. Even after 1975 only a very small growth in work force potential is initially expected.[17]

This superannuation is accompanied by a considerable surplus of women: at the end of 1968 there were about 9.3 million women and about 7.8 million men. This situation is reflected in the structure of the labor force: of the total working population of about 7.7 million in 1968, about 3.7 million or 50 per cent were females. Present trends clearly indicate a further increase in the percentage of female workers.

As of 1968, some 80 per cent of the total available work force were employed, for the most part as industrial and agricultural workers or white-collar employees. Thus, by the end of 1967, the SED's leadership had succeeded in putting an end to a steady drop in the absolute number of the employed, a trend which had begun in 1963. This was accomplished by the party mainly by recruiting from the available reservoir of housewives and pensioners, and, since 1963 particularly, an increasing number of

[18]

apprentices. However, despite these successes, the total number in the work force had by 1968 only reattained the 1960 figure.

The party's labor policies have also led to changes in the general occupational profile of the work force. In recent years, the number of those employed in blue-collar and white-collar positions has increased, both in relative and absolute terms. At the same time, the number of "self-employed" has fallen, in 1968 comprising only 0.2 per cent of the work force. Finally, the number of those employed in agriculture has steadily declined over the past few years; in 1968, they comprised only 12 per cent of the employed.

Changes in the occupational structure of the GDR's work force are generally comparable to those in the FRG.[18] However, the processes under way began later than they did in the FRG, since East Germany's economic reconstruction itself began some four or five years later than in West Germany.

Change permeates almost all segments of the social classes involved in the production process. An extraordinary horizontal and vertical mobility of numerous groups in the population has resulted. Three large social groups in particular have from the beginning been affected by SED mobilization pressures: the blue-collar workers, those employed in agriculture, and women.

If only for ideological and political reasons, the communists have since 1945 tried to enlist the support of the working class. In this effort they could fall back upon a social democratic as well as a communist tradition in parts of the working class in Saxony and Thuringia. It is all the more noteworthy, then, that the SED was for many years unsuccessful in its attempts to build up an elite class of workers — an effort which conformed to the party's ideological beliefs, but was not generally accepted. In fact, the traditional norms of society as a whole and the un-written party norms were on this point at almost diametrically opposite poles. Nor could they be reconciled in the newly developing social values of party and society. The "innovators" and the "worker researchers," who had since 1948 been depicted as heroic models, were not supported by the society as a whole. Such "models" were seen as forming a clique of workers who were loyal to the SED and who were specially assisted by the party for purely opportunistic and propagandistic purposes. (The most famous example of this phenomenon was the miner, Adolf Hennecke.[19])

Since the beginning of the sixties, the party's efforts in this direction have met with more success. Thus, the programs for the retraining of the working class (*Qualifizierungsbewegung*), designed to update the workers' qualifications to deal with more modern machines and production methods, have had some favorable results. Begun in 1960 under a Council of Ministers decree, retraining programs have been established and administered either by the industrial enterprises involved or by individual villages; by various mass organizations involved in production, such as the FDGB; and by higher technical institutions. In 1966 similar "refresher" courses for top industrial executives, undersecretaries of state, and higher party functionaries were initiated at the Central Institute for Socialist Economic Management in East Berlin.

On the whole, the relative success of this movement may be attributed to the fact that numerous re-qualification courses — given in factory-run schools, in trade and higher technical schools, and in primary schools, etc. — have been accessible to ambitious and hard-working young workers. In addition, job requirements and goals were very clearly formulated by the State Planning Commission in hundreds of occupational profiles. Hard work was rewarded by job promotion, which promised concomitant social advancement. Today there is no doubt that, for thousands of workers organized in the SED, the party hierarchy provides only the external framework for social advancement. Opportunities for upward mobility are further enhanced by the fact that, as a result of the refugee movement, a shortage of workers prevails. For this reason even unskilled workers change jobs frequently. Empirical studies made in 1963 and 1964 demonstrate that certain chemical concerns, assembly enterprises, and factories with a large percentage of female workers have been greatly affected by this increased mobility of workers.[20]

A similar situation prevails among former farmers and among agricultural workers. Here, as collectivization brought with it the industrialization of agriculture and the introduction of industrial management practices in the large agricultural co-ops, the party has introduced new jobs and new qualifications. For example, such specialities as tractor driver and agricultural accountant, among many others, have resulted in the upgrading of qualifications among agricultural workers. Thus, after years of failure, the party has finally succeeded in raising the pro-

[20]

ductivity of agricultural labor. This success is, however, a qualified one, since the skilled agricultural workers move to the city more often than the unskilled. Thus migration from the country to the city, especially among young people, is assuming large dimensions.[21]

The adequate incorporation of women into the work force has always encountered much larger obstacles. Women are more often family-oriented and more hesitant in seeking occupational advancement than the party would wish. This lack of enthusiasm for an outside occupation is understandable, because while in theory all doors are open to the occupational emancipation of women, in reality their employment opportunities are limited. The conservative, patriarchal strain in society, which also persists in many other areas, is obviously a factor here. In 1966 about 41 per cent of all those working in industry were women, but they occupied only 8.7 per cent of the leadership positions.[22]

The New Managers

With all this change, a new elite social group has developed, composed of the young managers and technocrats who run the numerous enterprises and large-scale corporations. It is one of the achievements of the "new economic system" that managers and technocrats can in the sixties find job satisfaction in state enterprises much more easily than was possible in the fifties. The reintroduction, in 1963, of the title of "general director" epitomizes the establishment of a rigid, hierarchical, management structure, based on the performance principle. These "general directors" were the leaders of the eighty or so Associations of State-Owned Enterprises (VVBs) which existed at the time (today there are about 110). From 1963 on, one also hears of "socialist trusts" in the GDR — a term which, in the long history of the German workers' movement, had never been used positively, "trusts" having for decades been the epitome of exploitation by capitalist entrepreneurs. It seems noteworthy that even in marxist semantics sacred shibboleths can be discarded.

Of more practical importance are the new decision-making opportunities which were in 1963 granted to managers in industry: they now participate actively in determining policies on new capital spending and investment, determinations based solely on increasing efficiency in a planning framework which is only loosely determined; they make suggestions for the pricing of

products; they are privy to technological planning and development in the area of their trust; and they are responsible for the
independent establishment of contacts with firms in other East
European countries as well as in the West, and for the recruitment of cadres in their branches of industry.

The phenomenon of a new elite group in industry and the
economy indicates perhaps most clearly that a unique "career
society" is developing in the GDR. The younger managers and
technocrats usually study some three to five years at one of the
famous technical colleges or business administration schools in
the GDR, such as the Technische Universität, in Dresden, the
Bergakademie Freiberg, the Technische Hochschule, in Ilmenau,
and the Hochschule für Okonomie, in Berlin. The following subjects are taught in the course of study, the quality of which has
been considerably improved in the last few years: the sociology of
organization, the theory of decision-making, operations research,
mathematics, cybernetics, electronic data-processing, social psychology, industrial and labor sociology, pedagogy, and a somewhat new interpretation of marxist philosophy and political
economy. Practical instruction in the form of case studies takes
up about 25 per cent of study time.[23] Before these courses of study
were established, the educational principles of some business
schools and managerial training programs in the United States
were carefully studied. In addition, the postgraduate training of
leaders is now continued at regular intervals, in centrally organized courses for further education at selected VVBs. The Central
Institute for Socialist Economic Management in East Berlin,
mentioned earlier, was designed specifically for this purpose by
the Central Committee of the SED.

After a three-to-four year course of study and an above-
average grade in examination, trainees can immediately find
positions as managerial assistants in large-scale enterprises or as
leading functionaries in central or district economic organs. Upon
the trainee's successful completion of a probationary period, the
way is open to a director's chair or to a leading post in the state
economic bureaucracy. It is not unusual for plant managers or
technical and sales managers in GDR enterprises to be only
thirty to thirty-five years old. In 1966, of thousands of plant
managers working in the 110 VVBs, 35 per cent had a diploma
from a university or technical college and 55 per cent had a
diploma from a higher technical school.[24] The political pre-

[22]

requisite for such a career is party membership. Further "commitment" is, however, rarely required of trainees qualified in technology and economics. Through such purely professional incentives the SED leadership has bound part of the youth to the destiny of the party and the state.

Consumption Patterns

Since 1964, the supply of consumer goods has improved steadily.[25] Private consumption has however increased more slowly than the growth rate of the economy as a whole. Thus, from 1963 to 1968, industrial production grew by about 37 per cent, while the growth rate in private consumption came to only about 20 per cent. The per capita consumption of higher-priced food stuffs has however increased since 1960.[25a] The same is true of per capita consumption of expensive luxury items.[25b] In addition, there also seems to have been some change in the use of more durable goods.[26]

The situation with respect to the supply of durable consumer goods has been complicated. While television sets, refrigerators, and washing machines are now very much more available, the comparable figures for automobiles are low (1960: 3.2 automobiles for each 100 households; 1967: 11.0). Although the relative increase in the supply of automobiles was high, the absolute increase was small: for each 1,000 people there were only five more automobiles in 1967 than in 1966. Nevertheless, automobiles are tending to replace mopeds, motor-scooters, and motorcycles. This is part of the general tendency toward the disappearance of lower quality goods from the market and toward an increase in the supply of durable consumer goods, even if the rate of increase is slow. In the case of certain goods such as television sets, one can already see a tendency to glut the market.

The Family Structure

The breakdown of the family unit or the loss of its socialization function are symptomatic of most highly industrialized societies. These universally recognizable tendencies have been intensified in the GDR by several other social and political factors — the pronounced incorporation of married women into the work force and the shifting of the educational function away from the family.

[23]

In 1966, in over 70 per cent of all married couples in the GDR, both husband and wife were working. One year later, in 1967, 70 per cent of all mothers with one child, 64 per cent of those with two children, and 55 per cent of those with three children were employed.[26a] This means that the educational function of the family has more and more been shifted to social institutions and organizations such as nurseries, kindergartens, schools, the Young Pioneers (*Junge Pioniere*), Free German Youth, and the Society for Sport and Technology. For this reason two of its most important functions — the status orientation of the child and the social control of members of a family over each other — have, at least in part, been shifted away from the family.

On the other hand, the new Family Law, which came into operation in April 1966, shows that the SED has practically eradicated the hostile attitude toward the "bourgeois" family which has deep roots in socialist and communist traditions. Thus, the Preamble to the Code of Family Laws specifically states that: "The family is the smallest unit of society. It is based on marriage contracted for life and on the especially close ties which arise from the emotional relationship between man and wife and the relationships of mutual love, respect and mutual trust among all members of the family." Here the family is recognized as the basic social unit of the society. One should nevertheless be aware of the fact that pressure for the occupational training of married women as well as for the "socialist" education of children has continually mounted. The codification of these socio-political measures can be found in the new Family Law, especially in Articles 10 (Paragraph 2), 42 (Paragraph 4), and 44.

In addition, numerous measures of the state's policy toward families have doubtless influenced the structure of the family — even if they cannot be considered "anti-family" in a strict sense. Thus, in the GDR the average marriage age for both sexes is lower than in the FRG. The lowering of the majority age to eighteen and the relatively high income of young people are probably equally responsible for this. However, the number of marriages has since 1961 diminished, while the number of divorces has since 1965 increased — with legal divorce regulations playing no small part in this. While in 1961 there were about 169,438 marriages and about 26,114 divorces, this relationship had by 1967 changed unfavorably for marriages, with 117,146 marriages and 28,303 divorces.[27]

[24]

As in other industrial societies, the tendency to have small families with one or two children has also become prevalent. Out of a total of 4.8 million households, there are children under seventeen in 2.4 million. In 1.2 million of these households, there is only one child; 0.7 million contain two children; and there are three or more children in only 0.5 million households. These figures clearly demonstrate a decline in the number of larger families, with four or more members.[28] A certain retreat into private family life may accompany this development.

Youth and the Performance Principle

Of course, the position of youth in an industrial society is complex. Therefore, only a few general remarks on this subject can be made here. In the GDR, youth is career-oriented. For the most part, it has avoided direct ideological indoctrination. The SED and the state have both provided substantial incentives for career-orientation. In the Youth Law of 1963, for example, the performance principle, which had previously been very much disputed, was very clearly and definitely stated.[29] A tendency toward encouraging functional specialization and efficiency, which lay at the heart of the "new economic system," should also not be overlooked.

If the performance principle was to be applied, a new admissions policy at the universities, the technical colleges, and the schools was required. That such a policy was introduced is clear from a comparative statistical evaluation of the social origin of students at such institutions, viewed in 1960 and 1967. (See Tables 1 and 2.)

At first glance one notes that the proportion of workers' children in the regular course of study at both universities and schools has diminished considerably. Only in the correspondence and evening divisions has there been a slight increase in workers' children enrolled in universities. The proportion of children from families of white-collar employees, the intelligentsia, and members of production co-ops who are studying fulltime at the universities and technical colleges and schools has, however, risen. This increase reflects the social consolidation of these classes. The comparative figures in the "correspondence and evening study" column should also be noted. For white-collar employees, a fairly high rate of increase is shown in technical and trade schools, while the percentage of students from white-collar backgrounds

[25]

Table 1

SOCIAL ORIGIN OF STUDENTS AT
UNIVERSITIES AND TECHNICAL
COLLEGES (*Hochschulen* AND
Fachhochschulen)*
(in percentages)

	FULLTIME STUDENTS		CORRESPONDENCE AND EVENING STUDENTS	
	1960	1967	1960	1967
Blue-collar workers	50.3	38.2	7.3	11.9
White-collar employees	19.2	23.5	61.8	30.8
Members of production co-ops	4.2	7.8	0.8	1.8
Intelligentsia	15.6	20.4	27.9	53.8
Self-employed	8.0	7.1	2.0	1.4
Other	2.7	3.0	0.2	0.3

Source: *Statistisches Jahrbuch der Deutschen Demokratischen Republik, 1968,* p. 473.

* The *Hochschulen* and *Fachhochschulen* totaled 44.

Table 2

SOCIAL ORIGIN OF STUDENTS
IN TECHNICAL AND TRADE
SCHOOLS (*Fachschulen*)*
(in percentages)

	FULLTIME STUDENTS		CORRESPONDENCE AND EVENING STUDENTS	
	1960	1967	1960	1967
Blue-collar workers	58.4	52.0	43.5	31.0
White-collar employees	18.6	20.5	41.6	61.2
Members of production co-ops	9.3	11.7	8.7	5.1
Intelligentsia	5.9	8.9	3.1	1.9
Self-employed	6.8	4.9	2.0	0.3
Other	1.0	2.0	1.1	0.5

Source: *Statistisches Jahrbuch der Deutschen Demokratischen Republik, 1968,* p. 470.

* The *Fachschulen* totaled 256 in 1960 and 188 in 1967.

studying parttime at universities has decreased from 61.8 to 30.8 per cent.

As is usual with statistics in the GDR, white-collar employees are not differentiated further. Knowledge of existing social mobility allows us to conclude, however, that children of higher salaried

[26]

personnel are today more able to complete the regular course of study at a university or college. Children of salaried personnel of middle or lower rank are, however, still very much dependent on correspondence and evening courses and also on evening trade schools for their education. Also striking is the great increase of students whose families are considered of the intelligentsia — especially in correspondence and evening courses at universities and colleges. The long-standing discrimination against this social class is visibly decreasing.

Planning and control of the curriculum have been accompanied by a normalization of admissions policies and a gradual abolition of the "class struggle" at the universities, colleges, and schools. However, we are unable to say how many young people, in accordance with the wishes of the SED or of the *Freie Deutsche Jugend* (FDJ), must study in fields which they did not choose. It is clear that indirect influence on the choice of the course of study continues to be applied systematically, especially in the primary schools and in the FDJ. Career planners are especially interested in young people with strong grounding in science and in the technical and medical professions. Recently, in line with the growing differentiation of the economic and legal system, lawyers and economists have also become increasingly needed. Finally, the GDR has had a perennial and acute shortage of teachers: nearly one-third of all new admissions to institutions of higher learning are therefore in the field of pedagogy. In contrast, there are relatively few current admissions in the fields of philosophy, philology, music, art, and theology. (See Table 3.)

Several other characteristics of the education of youth should be briefly indicated. The disparity between the occupational desires of young people and the needs of the national economy is a major aspect of the present situation. While in industry and agriculture it is specialized workers and technical engineers who are in greatest demand, young people often wish to enter those fields which enjoy the greatest prestige in the GDR. Thus, for example, it was determined in 1965 that the overwhelming majority of a random sample of non-student girls wanted to become salesgirls, cosmeticians, hairdressers, and seamstresses, and to go into all kinds of office work.[30] In contrast to the FRG, the jobs of nursemaid and teacher also enjoy prestige in the GDR.

Similarly, the SED is not pleased with the migration of youth

Table 3

FULLTIME AND PARTTIME SUDENTS AND
NEW ADMISSIONS, IN REGULAR
AND CORRESPONDENCE COURSES AT
UNIVERSITIES AND TECHNICAL
COLLEGES IN 1968

	TOTAL NUMBER	NEW ADMISSIONS
Mathematics and Natural Science	10,015	2,757
Engineering and Technology	28,617	7,070
Agriculture, Forestry, Veterinarian Medicine, and Food Stuffs	7,276	1,717
Medicine	10,404	1,516
Economics, Law, and Journalism	18,091	4,333
Philosophy, Linguistics, History, Esthetics, and Musicology	2,908	668
Art	1,797	466
Physical Education	1,171	265
Theology	576	124
Pedagogy (Education and Psychology)	29,726	7,880
Total	110,581	26,796

Source: *Statistisches Jahrbuch der Deutschen Demokratischen Republik, 1969,* pp. 389 ff.

from the country to the city.[31] As has been empirically demonstrated, the relatively poor educational opportunities in the countryside, the cultural differences between the city and the country, and the influence of the farmer-parents who now work in the LPGs, all play an essential role in this migration.

In numerous recent studies of youth, it has been made clear that the youth of the GDR is career-oriented and family conscious: "Many consider work and study to be central values. They seek professional satisfaction; they want to become qualified, to accomplish something which will make it possible for them to help others. It is emphasized over and over again that they would like their work to be useful to the society or to 'other people.' This ideal is widespread." [32]

This is also true of girls: their occupations take a central place in their lives. In various surveys, which have been reexamined and collated by W. Friedrich, over 70 per cent said they intended to undertake a permanent profession or one that would be only occasionally interrupted.[33] In a group of 209 girls, the following motives and views on work were advanced: a profession is a life task (36 per cent); a particular profession is considered inherently interesting (23 per cent); educational and vocational training would otherwise be wasted (15 per cent); particular work would serve the country and society (11 per cent); a desire to be independent (14 per cent); to support one's parents or husband, or to buy durable goods (12 per cent); general usefulness (13 per cent); and other reasons (6 per cent).

A New National Consciousness?

In most people who live in the GDR one cannot find a "national" or "exclusivist" consciousness of being a citizen of the GDR. The gap between the two parts of Germany has nevertheless grown wider and the "self-awareness" of numerous groups of working people has in the last few years increased. This has been almost in spite of the fact that — in contrast to the other East European countries — no independent national consciousness has been permitted to develop in the GDR. (In Poland, for example, nationalism — partly religious in motivation — has served almost as a connecting link between party and population.) In the GDR many people are now faced with the problem of developing a political identity.

The traditional norms of numerous social groups, which are for various reasons important to the party, originated in the totally different social system of pre-1945 Germany. The social norms which may be called traditional became relevant to the ruling SED from 1945 on, when large masses of these groups (such as laborers, farm workers, intellectuals, new and old style farmers, white-collar employees, and certain groups of artisans, small tradesmen, and small businessmen) entered the party and thus in 1945–1946 contributed decisively to the moulding of its character. In the first few years after 1945, various slogans, such as antimilitarism, pacifism, anti-capitalism, and humanism, were not simply the propaganda devices of the communists and former social democrats. They were inherent in the behavior patterns of important, politically active segments of the population. Such patterns did not however become an integral part of behavior patterns consistent with SED goals. It therefore became important for the SED to try to introduce a system of new legal norms.

Up to the present, professional and social advancement has provided the only road for the integration of a broader segment

[29]

of the population into the new system. It is therefore not surprising that the party has supported individual aspirations for advancement. Not without success, SED propagandists have tried to pass off a mixture of certain parts of the Prusso-German tradition, the heroic phase of communism, and the people's efforts at reconstruction over a twenty-year period (and their achievements as well) as a specific "GDR-consciousness." As a result, self-awareness, a pride in achievement, and scepticism toward the West and especially toward West Germany, have developed in large parts of the population, especially in the youth. An increasing number of citizens are becoming aware of their own State, which they view as being independent of the Federal Republic and which they accept, though not totally without criticism.

On the other hand, the majority of the people has always been very conscious not only of the Western (West German) standard of living but also of the Western style of living. Continuing shortages, especially in luxury items, are attributed to the comparatively poor economic situation in the GDR. This is one of the reasons why the persistent SED claim, that the "real" economic miracle in Germany is in East Germany, is neither totally believed nor totally accepted.

However, unless all available indicators are misleading, the SED may, in another decade, be more or less successful in convincing millions of economically active young people that "one can also live well in the GDR." The consciousness of a common German history and the superiority of a "democratic Germany" will perhaps not be lost on those who are now from twenty-five to thirty-five years old. But even assuming a continuation of a steady economic upswing in the GDR, this consciousness will probably not be stronger than the consciousness of the fact that two independent German states and social systems resulted from World War II and that they must be respected as such.

II

CHANGES IN THE SED (1958–1967) AND THE
EMERGING FACTIONS IN THE POLITBURO

Thus far, we have not treated the Socialist Unity Party (SED) as an essential part of GDR society nor have we considered changes within the party. Such changes are basically the concern of political sociology, which is not primarily focussed upon changes in methods of rule but tries to base the analysis of political change on measurable social data. So far as the SED is concerned, the political sociologist is naturally more interested in the occupational mobility of party leaders, their individual mobility patterns, problems of training the coming generation at all levels, and conflicts between role and social norms within the party. Such a perspective has the advantage of highlighting the fact that trends in the party mirror trends in society. The party must, in a certain sense, be a part of the society. Authority must not be regarded as something independent and isolated, but only as one of many interconnected factors. We side with those who believe that the functioning of society, with its "old" and "new" forms of cooperation as well as its tensions and conflicts, does in fact influence the actions and reactions of the party leadership. This would certainly seem true for the SED, given the fact that the party confronts a dynamic industrial society very different from the agricultural East Germany of the Soviet Occupation Zone (1945–1949).

In no other society in the Socialist Bloc — except perhaps for the Soviet Union — could the political elite play so prominent a role in the guidance and control of the entire economy and society as in the GDR. This has many historical reasons. Of all the leadership groups in East Europe those in the GDR could least trust those whom they ruled. They had originally come to power in a country which had lost the war and had been partitioned. The uprising in June 1953 was evidence that many people were not happy, and that, indeed, they were deeply

[31]

discontented with the SED's type of rule. A number of years later, in fact until the construction of the Wall in August 1961, many of those living in the GDR still hoped for reunification, not to speak of the collapse or restriction of the SED's authority. Their despair, hate, or dissatisfaction may have been partly reflected in the high numbers of refugees. A strong party "hand" was therefore essential.

In addition, the SED leadership had to modernize a society whose population was highly impressed by its dynamic "sister" industrial society, which had, in an incredibly short time, become prosperous. Beyond that, more than other party leaders in East Europe, the SED had to take account of the economic development of the USSR. Therefore it is not surprising that — after all political alternatives had been eliminated — the SED itself became the most important initiator of the process of change and modernization in the GDR. It has endeavored to carry out this task. How it has done so can be seen, in part, in the party's implementation of its compulsory collectivization policy and the "industrialization of agriculture."

If we are to see the most important characteristics of the SED's social structure more clearly, we must make a somewhat closer analysis of its social composition and of social change in the party. One should start with the changes which have taken place in both GDR society and the SED, especially since 1963. In his famous speech at the Sixth Party Congress of the SED, Ulbricht himself opened the door, as it were, for young, well-educated party workers to attain positions of leadership.[34]

We feel that a detailed sociological analysis, if possible, could prove that the process of a comprehensive mobilization and modernization of German society, which was begun under the national socialist party's rule, has since 1945 continued under the SED. Similar pressures for mobilization and modernization are still being applied today. Since, as the leading component of its society, the SED is *ipso facto* not excluded from the processes of social change, social mobility, and modernization, it must often also reflect these changes: thus, to a certain degree our statements about the SED pertain to the society as a whole.

Changes in the Social Composition of the SED

The SED is today both a cadre and mass party, headed by an exclusive oligarchy. As we have been using the term, the leadership groups in 1969 consisted of the following: the Politburo,

[32]

which had fifteen members and six candidates; the Secretariat of the Central Committee, consisting of ten secretaries; and the Central Committee, which contained one hundred and thirty-one members and fifty candidates. There are also some 70,000 SED functionaries, of whom about 2,000 are active in the central apparatus of the Central Committee. The others are divided among the following organizations: the fifteen secretariats of the SED *Bezirk* executives and their bureaucracies, the approximately two hundred secretariats of the SED *Kreis* executives, and other institutions under the aegis of the Central Committee or having some official party function, such as party training schools. In addition, there are some 120,000 propagandists.[35]

In 1945 the Communist Party of Germany (KPD) was primarily a classic cadre party. In 1946 it merged with the East German section of the Social Democratic Party (SPD) to form the Socialist Unity Party (SED). The result was a mass party which by the end of 1948 had 2 million members. In 1966, after a number of purges from 1948 to 1958, involving hundreds of thousands of former Social Democrats, the SED had about 1.8 million members. Thus, by 1966, the membership had again risen practically to its peak of 1948. The percentage of party members in the population had also increased, coming in 1969 to about 10 per cent. There is no doubt that the new Statute of

Table 4

SOCIAL COMPOSITION OF SED
MEMBERSHIP IN 1966

CLASS	NUMBER	PER CENT
Blue-collar workers	807,312	45.6
White-collar employees	285,066	16.1
Intelligentsia	217,796	12.3
Pensioners	214,049	12.1
Co-op farmers	112,998	6.4
Housewives	77,121	4.4
Students and school pupils	28,323	1.6
Producers' co-ops	15,029	0.8
Independent artisans; gardeners; fishermen; tradesmen and businessmen in semi-state-owned enterprises	12,218	0.7

Source: *Protokoll der Verhandlungen des VII. Parteitages des SED . . . 1967*, vol. IV, p. 226.

[33]

1963 concerning membership was responsible for this increase, as it eased conditions for membership. Under its terms, any applicant could become a member of the SED after one year's candidacy. He needed only to be formally recommended by two people who had been members of the party for at least two years. Until 1963, admissions regulations had been both much more complicated and harder to meet.

The important thing to note here is that — in its social composition and the qualifications demanded of its members — the SED has itself followed the trends of its society.[36]

Our knowledge about statistics of this kind is very limited. We do not know the exact criteria which were applied to the classifications. Which category, for example, includes the functionaries in the SED, the state, and the apparatus of the mass organizations? There is also confusion about the time when the individual party member was included in these statistics. Was he a "blue-collar worker" when entering the party or at the end of 1966? Was he included in this category on the grounds of his actual profession or his acquired profession? Thus, only tentative statements can be based on these statistics. Compared with the statistics for the end of 1961, the proportion of blue-collar workers is conspicuously high, since in 1961 the blue-collar percentage was only 33.8. The same holds for the intellectuals, who were in 1961 represented by only 8.7 per cent. On the other hand, the percentage of "white-collar employees" decreased between 1961 and 1966, from 32.6 per cent to 16.1 per cent, while the percentage of co-op farmers remained nearly the same, at 6.2 per cent in 1961 and at 6.4 per cent in 1966.

The workers, intelligentsia, and employees form the basis of the party. The proportion of co-op farmers in the SED is by comparison negligible. The government seeks to underline the party's character as a workers' party by stressing the view that intellectuals and employees are also workers, though white-collar ones, or by indicating that they were workers when they entered the party.

We may conclude from the above that qualified people have increasing access to power in the SED. This fact becomes even more evident when one considers that, by the end of 1967, approximately 250,000 members or roughly 14 per cent of the SED had already completed a course of study at a university or technical college or a trade school.[37]

The rising proportion of professionally qualified SED members continues as a parallel to the tendency of the party to include increasing numbers of younger people in its ranks. At the end of December 1966, the composition of the SED by age groups was as follows: [38]

Twenty-five and younger	145,121 or	8.2 per cent
From 26 to 30	214,527 or	12.1 per cent
From 31 to 40	443,384 or	25.1 per cent
From 41 to 50	305,217 or	17.2 per cent
From 51 to 60	286,079 or	16.2 per cent
From 61 to 65	147,304 or	8.3 per cent
Over 65	228,280 or	12.9 per cent

By contrast, in 1950 only 11 per cent of the party's members were from 26 to 30 years of age. The comparable figure for those from 31 to 40 years of age was 18.7 per cent.[39] Especially striking is the disproportionately high percentage of party members in the age groups from 31 to 40, who now comprise more than one-fourth of the total SED membership. Consequently, at least numerically, this age group plays an important role in the party, as it does in other areas of the society, notably in the economy. This had not been the case in earlier years.

Changes in the Organizational Structure

Structural changes in SED organization came hand in hand with changes in the membership structure. These innovations may be briefly characterized as a further extension of traditional organization principles. Until 1963 the party was organized on the so-called "territorial" principle. In this system, the chain of command extended from the supreme party bodies at the center down the party hierarchy through the *Kreis* level. This principle may in our terminology be equated with the so-called "line principle" of organization. Later, after 1963, the "production principle," which divides the party apparatus along functional production lines, was also adopted. The most important production sectors were: industry, construction, agriculture, and ideology. In the form in which the production principle was introduced in the GDR in 1963, the production sectors were combined with the territorial organs, i.e., the production sectors were organized on the *Bezirk* and *Kreis* levels. Applying Western concepts, especially those of industrial sociology, one might characterize

[35]

the changes in the organizational system of the SED as follows: the line organizational component was complemented by staff or functional organization. In 1963 "staffs" were, in this sense, added to existing line party organs on all levels of the party organization (the state or central level, the *Bezirk*, and the *Kreis* levels).

The work of these staffs was concentrated functionally in industry and construction, agriculture, agitation, and ideology. Of course, there have been further changes in the party apparatus since 1963, but the functional principle has been retained. The newly created staffs were manned by younger, more specialized, functionaries, who had in most cases successfully completed technical or economic programs of study. The task of these staffs consisted primarily of establishing working contacts within the network of the party organization in enterprises, economic management, and party organizations at the *Bezirk* and *Kreis* levels. They were entrusted the task of ensuring that resolutions in the economic realm of the Politburo and of the SED Central Committee were realized more quickly and effectively than heretofore. In addition, the newly instituted staffs were designed to improve the flow of information and communication both within the economy and between economic entities and the party. The staffs actually fulfilled these tasks much better than had earlier organizational forms, which had been run by *apparatchiki* schooled solely in "agitprop" and other ideological mobilizational activities.

The innovations heralded by the introduction of the production principle shook the entire party apparatus. Previously, party organs at all levels had been concerned purely with safeguarding political power. The political, economic, and social instability of the system was reflected in this exclusive concern. In 1963 a general shift from political to economic concerns could be seen in the SED: party organs began to deal increasingly with purely economic matters. To be sure, the Politburo had announced this goal as early as 1952. Its realization was, however, years in coming. The development of an economic system which was both functional and competitive required a type of organization different from the one which had aimed at establishing security and legitimizing power. Above all, the realization finally took hold in the Politburo of the SED that in an industrial society political and technical know-how tended not to go together. As the example of the Soviet Union demonstrated, only in its

[36]

revolutionary, earlier phases can a movement expect that political and technical know-how would be effectively combined in a single person or organization. In a more dynamic, differentiated system, it is hard to coordinate technical-functional and ideological-political authority in one authoritative body — much less in one person. It was in particular Ulbricht who, by his policy (in 1963) of more or less "open admission" to both the Central Committee and the Politburo, succeeded in holding the "political" and "economic" factions of the party together. It is true that this policy was in 1965 followed by a more conservative political line. Evidently, at the time, the authority of the party leadership needed to be strengthened.

At this point one naturally wonders as to the political consequences of such a party remodelling of organization and membership both. One may with confidence assume that the most sweeping overall change — that is, the reorganization and professionalization of SED membership — has led to new conflicts within the party apparatus. How have these, to start with latent, internal conflicts finally been politically manifested?

For our purposes, we may separate out three major types of this sort of conflict. First, within the SED there is now a generation gap comparable to that in the society as a whole. The widening of this gap has had its own peculiar and important ramifications in the party. Secondly, we can detect a tension between the "problem-solving" outlook of the party experts and the views of the primarily political party functionaries who do not possess particular technical expertise. Fnally, the increasing professionalization of SED membership has led to organizational conflicts of interest among the various bureaucracies of the party, the state, and the economy. The SED leadership has had to cope with these problems. Up to now they have — thanks to Walter Ulbricht's tactical flexibility — succeeded in integrating these conflicts and thus preventing them from becoming dysfunctional.

Party Training

In 1965, after a delay of two years, the requirements of the "new economic system" were applied to the training of the SED cadres. In the Politburo decision on cadre policy, of February 17, 1965, two new demands were made of leading party cadres:

> For one thing, they must have at their disposal more specialized knowledge and experience in the area for which they are

responsible or in which they work; secondly, each party functionary must have solid knowledge and ability in the area of leadership — i.e., he must familiarize himself more and more with the scientific fundamentals of working with people, with the sociology of organization, as well as with modern technical means and methods of management and of human relations. This should also include the acquisition of basic knowledge in the area of projective planning, management, and organization and a familiarity with network techniques, operations research, information theory, electronic data-processing, etc., as well as knowledge in the fields of pedagogy, sociology, psychology, and knowledge of the role and significance of cybernetics and its major uses in management.[40]

We should add that all the younger cadres are also required to specialize in a specific area of economics, law, engineering, or allied fields. Since mid-1965, instruction in such fields has been given on all levels of party training — even if, depending on the individual party school — it may be non-intensive. In this connection, the *Kreis* as well as the *Betrieb* schools of marxism-leninism, which exist in all SED *Kreis* executive bodies as well as in the party directorates in the big enterprises and "socialist trusts," are of particular importance. According to the most recent data, there are now about 450 such schools, with some 35,000 students.[41] This type of course lasts for a year and the students usually attend while continuing their jobs.

The next level of party training involves the so-called "special schools" for SED *Bezirk* executives, of which there are now twenty-five, with room for from 2,500 to 3,000 students. These institutions offer an intensive three-month supplementary course of study designed for party secretaries in enterprises and VVBs and for other leading functionaries on the *Bezirk* level. The special schools also give short, two-week courses. In addition to these schools, there are *Bezirk* party schools headed by *Bezirk* executives, which offer one-year courses to selected personnel.[42]

At the top of the pyramid are the Karl Marx Party Academy and the Institute for Social Sciences, the latter set up in East Berlin by the Central Committee of the SED. Both institutions resemble universities closely, with both teaching and research functions. The Party Academy is open to members and candidates of the Central Committee, secretaries of *Bezirk* and *Kreis* executives, teachers at party schools, and to leading functionaries of the state apparatus, the economy, and mass organizations. Its courses last for three years and end with an examination which, if successfully completed, leads to a degree in the social sciences (*Diplom-Gesellschaftswissenschaftler*). Attendance at the Central Committee's Institute for Social Sciences is restricted to persons already holding a degree in history, social science, law, economics, or psychology. Studies last four years and may lead to a doctorate (*Promotion*). Criteria for selecting students are strict: only future "leaders," who have already been well tested "in theory and practice," are admitted.

There is no doubt that the party's system of training has recently become more effectively organized and that the curricula are now better balanced. Thus, well-educated and versatile young functionaries, who are more able to cope with the problems of GDR society than were the subservient dogmatists of the fifties and early sixties, are appearing in increasing numbers in almost all areas of the economy and society. It will naturally be some time before these people occupy positions of political leadership and gain international prestige.

The Central Committee of the SED in Transition

We have already emphasized that the increase in younger members and the more frequent recruitment of specialists at the party's top levels are the two most important aspects of change in the SED. The increase in younger members and candidates and, also, the increasing professionalization of the party elite are quite obvious.[43] We shall treat the rejuvenation of the party at its upper levels first. (See Table 5.)

In the past ten years, roughly speaking, the number of persons in the Central Committee who are today from 30 to 50 years old has risen from 34 to 100. In the 1967 Central Committee those born between 1920 and 1939 were already in the majority, coming to 100 out of a total of 181 members and candidates. The younger age groups are distributed not only among candidates to the Central Committee (as was true in earlier years) but also comprise a considerable proportion of full members (61 out of 131 members of the 1967 Central Committee).

Clearly, the changes within the entire party are also distinctly reflected in its Central Committee. Since 1963 the number of younger graduates of universities, technical and other colleges, and trade schools among members and candidates of the Central

[39]

Table 5

MEMBERS AND CANDIDATES IN THE
CENTRAL COMMITTEE (CC) OF THE
SED BY AGE, FROM 1954 TO 1967

| | CC MEMBERS AND CANDIDATES, ELECTED AT THE | | | |
| | IV PARTY CONGRESS | V PARTY CONGRESS | VI PARTY CONGRESS | VII PARTY CONGRESS |
YEAR OF BIRTH	(1954)	(1958)	(1963)	(1967)
1890 and earlier	8	7	4	0
1890–1899	18	19	12	11
1900–1909	42	49	43	30
1910–1919	26	34	40	40
1920–1929	19	34	74	87
1930–1939	0	0	8	13
No data	22	12	0	0

Source: Peter C. Ludz, *Parteielite im Wandel*, pp. 163, 336.

Committee has also increased. At the same time, there is a tendency to dismiss those functionaries in the Central Committee who have had only an elementary school education. The younger members of the Central Committee are for the most part in technical and economic and leading administrative positions. In addition, the spectrum of professions represented in the Central Committee has been considerably expanded.

For their part, representatives of the younger generation, who are, mainly, the managers and technocrats within the party, now more readily accept their association with the SED as an opportunity for professional and general social advancement, since there is a tendency in the GDR to reward every concrete achievement. In addition, opportunities for advancement have been expanded. The upward social mobility of the new elite has by no means taken place solely within the party hierarchy, but also in the various state and economic bureaucracies. In addition, changes in the promotion and demotion processes can also be observed: the professional and political advancement (or demotion) of members of the party's leadership bodies are no longer necessarily inseparable. Especially important is the fact that loss of political function no longer automatically leads to loss of professional position, as it would have in earlier years.

Career Patterns

Generally speaking, four routes of advancement are available to members and candidates of the Central Committee or the Politburo: first, promotion within the SED; second, advancement within the state apparatus; third, advancement first in the party apparatus and then in the state apparatus; fourth, the reverse of the third career pattern.

On the basis of empirical analysis, it is clear that certain functional areas are relatively mutually self-exclusive — if we look at them in terms of the career patterns of Central Committee members. Traditional research on communist systems often maintains that positions in such a society are interchangeable. This would not seem to hold for the GDR, which is developing rather authoritarian forms of government: the ruling system, which is here, in accordance with Rensis Likert's term, denominated "consultative authoritarianism," involves a noteworthy proliferation of consultative and control bodies.[44] The number of persons active in these entities has accordingly risen. Increasing differentiation and specialization in organization necessitate special training programs and careers. Therefore, the members and candidates of the Central Committee may now be significantly differentiated by career pattern. It would seem that a functionary working in economics now would be much less interchangeable with a party functionary than would have been the case in the early fifties.

In this context, four individual careers of special political significance would seem worth examining: as an example of a younger specialist in the party apparatus, that of Günter Mittag; as an example of a younger specialist in a state apparatus, that of Werner Jarowinsky; as an example of a middle-aged party functionary pursuing a traditional path within the party, that of Erich Honecker; and as an example of a middle-aged party functionary on a traditional path within the state apparatus, that of Willi Stoph.

(1) *Günter Mittag*, member of the Politburo and Central Committee Secretary for Economic Affairs, was born in 1926 into a blue-collar worker's family. He was at first a skilled railroad worker, and later studied economics. He received his doctorate in economics in 1958. His specialty has been transportation problems. He has belonged to the SED since 1946. A functionary of the Central Committee of the SED since 1951, in 1954 he became the head of the section for transportation in the Central

[41]

Committee apparatus; from 1958 to 1961 he was Secretary of the Politburo Economic Commission, and, in 1961 and 1962, Deputy Chairman and Secretary of the National Economic Council, which was dissolved at the end of 1965. In 1958 Mittag also became a candidate member of the Central Committee; he has been a full member since 1962. Also in 1962 he took over the key position of Central Committee Secretary for Economic Affairs. Promoted to candidate's status in the Politburo, in 1963 he was designated head of the Politburo's newly established (and shortly thereafter dissolved) Bureau for Industry and Construction. As head of this bureau Mittag played an important role in pragmatic decision-making as well as in the successful realization of the "new economic system." In 1966 Mittag became a full member of the Politburo.

Although his professional career has been completely within the party, it has differed considerably from the traditional "purely party" career because Mittag has been able to get valuable experience in various responsible economic positions as well. Basically, however, his career is one-dimensional: he has always been an economic specialist and for a long time more of a transportation expert than an all-round economist. As a specialist in an area which has been a perennial bottleneck in the GDR, he became increasingly useful to the political leaders. He took advantage of this opportunity, and he could do so without apprehension, since he did not seek to compete with those in established positions.

(2) An example of the career of a young specialist in the state apparatus is that of *Werner Jarowinsky*, candidate to the Politburo and Central Committee Secretary for Trade and Supply. Born in 1927 to the family of an SPD functionary, Jarowinsky after the war first worked as a functionary in the FDJ and then in the People's Police. In 1945 he joined the German Communist Party, and in 1946 the SED. Jarowinsky studied economics and received his doctorate in 1956. First he became a leading functionary, then the director of the Research Institute in the Ministry of Trade and Supply, and in 1958 he became the head of a general division in this ministry. Since 1958 one of the deputies to the Minister, he in 1961 became Undersecretary and First Deputy to the Minister. Since 1963 he has been a full member of the Central Committee of the SED. In the same year he was named to Politburo candidate membership and appointed Central Committee secretary.

Jarowinsky's professional career pattern seems to be a proto-
type for at least one type of specialist in the SED: the specialist
who, after reaching a certain point, advances rapidly. Usually,
as in the case of Mittag and Jarowinsky, such men share a close
association with economic affairs. They have very little close
professional contact with the traditional party positions in the
area of party organization, agitprop, and ideology. For example,
Jarowinsky began to work his way up in 1958 by specializing in
the improvement of consumer goods' supply, at a time when this
problem had become politically relevant for the party.

(3) An example of the career of a middle-aged party functionary on the traditional path of advancement within the party
is *Erich Honecker*, member of the Politburo and Central Committee Secretary for Security, Military and Organizational and
Cadre Affairs. Born in 1912 and the son of a construction worker,
he first learned the trade of a tiler. By 1926 he was already a
member of the German Communist Youth Union (KJVD) and,
by 1929, of the German Communist Party. In 1931 he became
Secretary of the KJVD for the Saar area and, in 1934, a member
of its Central Committee. In 1935 Honecker was arrested by
the Nazis and sentenced to a ten-year prison term. In 1945 he
began to organize the Free German Youth (FDJ) in what was
then the Soviet Occupation Zone, and he was the chairman of
this mass organization for almost a decade (from 1946 to 1955).
In 1955–1956 he received additional political training in the Soviet
Union. Following this, he in 1958 became the Central Committee
secretary responsible for all questions of security and military
affairs. Since 1946 Honecker has also been a member of the
Party Executive Committee (later the Central Committee of
the SED). In 1950 he became a candidate and in 1958 a full
member of the Politburo.

In contrast to the careers of Mittag and Jarowinsky, Honecker's career is traditional. First a functionary in the communist youth organization, he reached the actual power center
of the party, though relatively late. The heavily ideological
concepts involved in problems of security, of the secret service,
and the National People's Army (NVA) have doubtless left a
deep imprint on his character.

(4) *Willi Stoph's* career may serve as an example of the
career of a middle-aged party functionary using a traditional
path of advancement in the state apparatus. Willi Stoph, member of the Politburo and Prime Minister of the GDR, was born

[43]

in 1914, the son of a worker. He learned the skill of bricklayer, entered the KJVD in 1928, and the KPD in 1931. He served in the army in a noncommissioned capacity from 1935 to 1937 and from 1939 to 1945. Immediately after the war, he joined the reconstituted KPD. First he was a higher functionary for the building industry in what was then the German Central Administration for Industry in the Soviet Occupation Zone. In view of his high positions immediately after the war, we may assume that he had become a protégé of the Soviets during his wartime internment in the USSR. In 1948 Stoph became the head of the SED Central Committee's Section for Economic Affairs. From 1951 to 1957 he headed the Bureau for Economic Affairs for the Prime Minister. From 1952 to 1955 he was Minister of Internal Affairs and Deputy Chairman of the Council of Ministers. In 1956 he became Colonel-General of the National People's Army and Minister for National Defense. In this capacity, he was decisive in building up the National People's Army. From 1960 on, as deputy to the Chairman of the Council of Ministers (Prime Minister), his duties were primarily to coordinate party and state decisions and to put them into effect in the economy. At Grotewohl's death in 1964, Stoph became Prime Minister and one of the deputy chairmen of the Council of State. As early as 1950 he had become a member of the Central Committee of the SED; he has been a full member of the Politburo since 1953.

Stoph's career can be characterized as traditional. In contrast to Honecker's career, however, Stoph's is more diversified because for the most part it has remained consistently within the state's economic and military apparatus. Stoph is, then, more versatile than Honecker and, on the whole, a personality that both radiates and wins more confidence. This must be taken into consideration so as not to overrate Honecker's relative position in the leadership.

One may ask how such career patterns are relevant to political analysis. Why are these biographical data important for understanding a political system? Empirical sociological analysis of career patterns within political elites not only indicates something about social change within the system but also sheds light on the velocity of such change. This is particularly evident when one considers the careers of the younger members of the SED leadership.

In an earlier study, the author referred to the younger mem-

[44]

bers of the Politburo, especially Günter Mittag and Werner Jarowinsky, as the nucleus of the "institutionalized counter-elite." [45] They are a "counter-elite" insofar as they share careers that contrast with those of the "old guard." An analysis of the younger mens' careers demonstrates that economic and technological know-how is in present-day communist systems an important avenue to political power. This group is a "counter-elite" also in the sense that it is often viewed with a certain mistrust by the established elite, the "apparatchiki," who consider them as representative of the experts and technocrats in the party.

This counter-elite is "institutionalized" in that it is firmly rooted in the party, state, and economic hierarchy. Its pragmatic criticism of particular decisions of the Politburo should not be misrepresented as a critique of the system or of its ideological foundations. The members of this group regard themselves as convinced marxists within the framework of the political system of the GDR. Yet, in contrast to that of many older functionaries, their marxism is not rigidly ideological. One could describe these younger SED leaders as pragmatically-oriented new conservatives, who stand in contrast to the more dogmatically-oriented old conservatives of the Honecker wing of the Politburo. All the spokesmen of this group advocate the continuation of the economic and technological modernization of the GDR. Thus — although primarily for pragmatic reasons — they support all those economic reforms which can improve the industrial and agricultural performance of the GDR and thus also increase its political strength.

Recent Conflicts in Leading Party Bodies

Basic conflicts in values within the SED have really only manifested themselves since the introduction of the "new economic system." Since that time, the style of life and work in the GDR has as a whole become more dynamic; the tempo, faster; and the necessity to inform oneself on major issues, greater. This has also been true, of course, for the SED. Used for many years to a slower work pace, many functionaries, and not only the older ones, adapted themselves to the new requirements only with great difficulty. Since 1963, the ideals represented by the younger experts and their pragmatic style of administration, which is at an opposite pole from the bureaucratism of the hard-core functionaries (apparatchiki), have achieved far greater prominence. The debates about the new leadership "style" within

[45]

the top reaches of the party have therefore become more and more bitter. Since we are dealing with the complex phenomenon of different conceptions of a correct *modus operandi* or "leadership style," a series of factors ought to be taken into consideration.

First, we should mention the generation conflict, which has considerable political significance today in all communist parties, in the West as well as the East. In the GDR, this conflict is complicated by two factors. The political conceptions, the ideals, the overall outlook of the younger specialists, technocrats, and managers stand in direct opposition to those of the hard-core old-timers. The representatives of the younger generation, economic experts like Günter Mittag and Werner Jarowinsky, the data-processing specialist Günther Kleiber, the agricultural expert George Ewald, grew up in the GDR after the war under a system ruled by a communist party already firmly in power. They have studied in the GDR and have, for the most part, completed technical or economic programs of study at one of the universities or technical colleges and have received diplomas or doctoral degrees. None of these men have been trained or re-trained in the Soviet Union. Furthermore, they have not undergone the ideological pressures associated with training in the Comintern schools. These men did not have to face the bitter fate of emigration either to the Soviet Union or to other countries. They did not suffer in the concentration camps of Hitler or Stalin. They have not fought in the International Brigades in the Spanish Civil War. And they did not have to denounce the ideals of their youth in a servile manner and adapt themselves to the manifold, highly fluctuating policies and tactics of a communist party fighting for power.

The young experts have been trained to transform a society already ruled by a communist party into a competitive, successful industrial country. Their energies did not have to be focused on the destruction of "bourgeois society" or on the continuous persecution of ideological "deviationist groups" within party ranks. They are therefore less enslaved within narrow boundaries of firmly established ideological doctrines, which allow one to differentiate only between "revolution" and "reaction," and "left" and "right sectarianism." Their day-to-day behavior shows that they attach less significance to ideological questions in politics. They are representatives of a more highly differentiated perspective — social engineers who are interested in reforms within

[46]

the system as it presently stands. For them "reform" means addressing themselves to the concrete problems of the society, especially its economic problems. The gap between the younger technocrats and society is, therefore, narrower than the one which separates that society from the older functionaries. Of course, the representatives of the younger generation in the leading bodies of the SED also consider themselves faithful marxists or communists. For this reason, there is still an open line of communication between traditional modes of thought and their own. Within the framework of the party, they may be called "neo-conservatives" — versatile, pragmatic individuals, eager to participate in important decisions. Whole worlds separate them from the dullness and inflexibility of the older functionaries.

A second factor which adds to the generation conflict within the SED involves the infiltration of new prestige and status rankings into the party proper. By this "infiltration" we mean specifically the high esteem in which "bourgeois efficiency" has in the last few years come to be held. In the past, the German Communist Party had consistently condemned job efficiency as a criterion for advancement and had reserved its rewards for talent in political organization, agitation, conspiracy, and, in particular, for skill in ideological discussion. Knowledge of mathematics, economics, and technology had not figured in its scale of rewards. Therefore most of the older functionaries are barely if at all acquainted with economic and social affairs and issues. But it is precisely in these fields that the younger functionaries show the most interest. However, meaningful discussion between the two groups on these subjects is difficult, since the older functionaries often hardly know how to formulate the points of departure for such discussion, which they tend to see in the inadequate terms of the communism of the twenties. Further exacerbating the situation is the fact that the older bureaucrats often do not see the necessity for pluralist incentives, initiatives, and controls. Thus, the younger pragmatists may be accused within their own party of being representatives not of a political but of an economic party.

It is difficult to predict the character of the concrete policies which the "Young Turks" of the SED would institute were they to accede to power. In all probability they would not attempt to alter the general contours of present domestic and foreign policies. However, they would probably strive to remodel the present

[47]

system so as to make it more efficient. They would probably also try to diminish long-lasting ideological tensions in the GDR as a whole and the present tensions between the two Germanies. Finally, to a much greater degree than the older generation of SED leaders, they would in all likelihood stress their past political and economic worth, to the USSR and to the other members of the Socialist Bloc. They would probably also try to make the GDR-USSR relationship much more one of equal partners than has so far been the case.

In addition to the generation conflict and the other factors which have a direct impact on it, further tensions within the SED should be mentioned briefly. These are all as much an expression of dynamic developments in the GDR as the reasons for their existence. In this context, conflicts over spheres of responsibility among the greatly enlarged bureaucracies in the party, state, and economy should be emphasized. These conflicts result from the unsatisfactory solution of the many problems in information and communication. Even the reform of the large bureaucracies which accompanied the "new economic system" has not resulted in the clear definition and demarcation of competence. Such rivalries have therefore increased rather than diminished since the start of the reforms.

Factions in the Politburo

At present writing, the SED Politburo, which is the highest decision-making body of the party, consists of twenty-one members and candidates. In contrast to the Central Committee, where the specialists have, especially from 1963 to 1966, made a large contribution to policy debate, political debate in the Politburo is much more of a closed affair and takes place in a body largely insulated from public scrutiny. But general tendencies within the society, the party, and the Central Committee are reflected even here. Various factions can be discerned in the SED's supreme body. In all likelihood they will play a major role in deciding on Ulbricht's successor.

The dominating figure in the SED Politburo has always been Walter Ulbricht, the elderly First Secretary of the Central Committee and Chairman of the Council of State. He has led the party without interuption since its formation in 1946. Typically, Ulbricht has relied on different groups within the shifting balance of power in the Politburo for support, and he has always been a master tactician in working with its various factions. As early as February 1958, after he had removed Zaisser and Schirdewan as rivals, Ulbricht had consolidated his preeminent position in the Politburo. At the beginning of 1963, after a long period of over-cautious waiting, he granted access to the upper hierarchical reaches of the SED to impatient young functionaries who had been waiting in the wings. This naturally brought him into conflict with the dogmatic core in the Politburo, (including Alfred Neumann and Paul Fröhlich). But at the beginning of 1964, when an over-zealous "technocracy" appeared to threaten a take-over of the party, Ulbricht began to realign himself with its conservative elements. He has remained true to this line in subsequent years, without however definitely breaking off his relations with the younger technocrats.

At the time of writing, perhaps most important in the Politburo is the group of flexible and diversified functionaries between the ages of fifty and sixty. These men have accumulated much varied experience in party work, in the state apparatus, in the economy, in the military, and in the communist youth organ-ization. Politically and ideologically they range from conservative to dogmatic, without, however, being inflexible. These func-tionaries advocate a policy proposed by Ulbricht since at least 1961: namely, that the GDR establish the closest possible links with the Soviet Union in all fields. Members of this group include the "crown princes" of the party, Erich Honecker (born in 1912) and Will Stoph (born in 1914), the SED's chief ideologist Kurt Hager (born in 1912), the hard-line but competent First Secretary of the SED *Bezirk*-Executive for (East) Berlin, Paul Verner (born in 1911), the First Secretary of the SED *Bezirk*-Executive for Halle, Horst Sindermann (born in 1915), and the Central Committee Secretary for Western Affairs and Propaganda, Hermann Axen (born in 1916).

In addition we find a group of younger functionaries who represent the technocrats and experts in the Politburo. Most prominent among them are economic specialists Günter Mittag (born in 1926) and Werner Jarowinsky (born in 1927), finance expert Walter Halbritter (born in 1915), agricultural specialists George Ewald (born in 1926) and Gerhard Grüneberg (born in 1921), and specialist in electronic data-processing Günther Kleiber (born in 1932). These functionaries are also flexible, but in a different sense than the older group we have mentioned.

[49]

While the flexibility of the former can be seen in their ideological interpretation of events, the flexibility of the latter manifests itself when it comes to the pragmatic solution of practical problems. Moreover, these younger technocrats have the advantage of being able to work pragmatically and of being located at the levers which actually guide the economic system. They see to it that the decisions of the Politburo are implemented in industrial concerns and in the local party organizations. At some later time, one might well expect new proposals concerning the "two Germanies" problem from this group, if, indeed, such proposals will be forthcoming from the present SED leadership at all.

A third group of functionaries in the Politburo is significant most of all simply for its firm faithfulness to Ulbricht. Politically, these functionaries have neither a general profile nor particular individual influence. Their conservative attitude and their inflexibility strengthen, *de facto*, the dogmatic wing within the Politburo. Among them we find long-time (till 1967) mayor of (East) Berlin, Friedrich Ebert (born in 1894), the head of the Party Control Commission, Hermann Matern (born in 1893), the long-time Chairman of the FDGB, Herbert Warnke (born in 1902), the First Secretary of the SED *Bezirk*-Executive for Frankfurt-on-the-Oder, Erich Mückenberger (born in 1910), and the agricultural functionary, Margarete Müller (born in 1931).

Finally, mention should be made of several older, particularly inflexible functionaries, who represent the "purist" dogmatic wing of the Politburo: Paul Fröhlich, the First Secretary of the SED *Bezirk*-Executive for Leipzig (1913–1970); Alfred Neumann, the First Deputy to the Chairman of the Council of Ministers (born in 1909); and Albert Norden, Central Committee Secretary for Agitation (born in 1904).

Two groups in the Politburo stand out as important to our analysis of change in the party and society: the younger technocrats and the experienced functionaries of the middle generation. Certain common traits can be attributed to both groups; an optimal combination of these traits will probably be decisive when it comes to selecting Ulbricht's successor. These factors are: trustworthiness in the eyes of the Soviet leaders; support from groups in the CPSU Central Committee; knowledge of the workings of the party apparatus, based on many years' experience; and a certain flexibility in solving different kinds of complicated problems in an "appropriate" way. By "appropriate," in this case, we mean in such a way as to both maintain the SED in power and meet and absorb the pressures from a socio-economically demanding and relatively stable but politically weak society. The perceptiveness needed to balance these two crucial considerations against one another is hard to attain.

None of the individual members of these two groups is, in our opinion, strong enough on his own merits to be considered a possible successor to Ulbricht. This also holds true for Honecker in our opinion. For this reason, it is more likely that after Ulbricht there will be a "triumvirate," composed of Honecker, Stoph, and Mittag. From the political standpoint as well, this triumvirate would represent the present alignment of power in the Politburo. It would also seem to represent a balance between the various "styles" of administration and leadership evident in the ruling body. To be sure, the time when the problem of Ulbricht's successor becomes acute may still be far off. All rumors notwithstanding, he seems to be ruling the GDR in as vigorous a style as ever.

Regardless of how the political factions align themselves after Ulbricht's retirement from power, the process of adaptation within the economy, within science, and within society as a whole, which has since 1963 been aimed at making the system more effective seems by now to be irreversible. Furthermore, the current loosening of the overly close dependence on Soviet policies, at least in domestic matters and especially in social policies, will probably not be reversed by any successive political leadership. On the other hand, the connection with the Soviet Union in foreign affairs and foreign trade will probably be consolidated further. Both dogmatists and reformers agree that the GDR can play a dominant role in the Eastern Bloc and in European politics only as a junior partner to the Soviet Union, though probably not as such a servile one as in the past. In this regard at least, the latitude in policy formation actually open to any new leadership is small. Differences from Ulbricht's policies will be found mainly in such domestic spheres as the style of the administration, the tempo of economic growth, and a greater receptivity to the wishes of the East German people. But, initially at least, any new regime will certainly not initiate any fundamental reorientation of policy, but will hew to the general lines established in the early 1960s by the Ulbricht regime.

[51]

III

WHY IS THERE NO POLITICAL CHANGE IN THE GDR?

In 1963–1964, various observers of the GDR expected that the economic reforms would sooner or later bring about basic political changes as well. They were fascinated by the prospect that dynamic economic changes might automatically set loose new forces in other areas of the society, especially in politics. Others believed that the economic reforms were themselves to be equated with political liberalization.

These vain hopes and false predictions were understandable, for the "professional pessimists" in the Federal Republic of Germany had for all too long predicted that everything would continue to go badly in the GDR. From a psychological point of view, the time for a basic reassessment seemed to have come. However, as so often happens, the reassessment went too far. Since the GDR had for so long enjoyed such low repute in the FRG and elsewhere in the West, observers have in recent years tended to exaggerate the potential for economic and educational modernization in East Germany.[46]

In starting to discuss the question of why there is and has been no political change in the GDR, we should first of all make clear what we mean by the term "change." Change is a sociological concept as well as one in general use in the social sciences. In research about Eastern Europe, this term serves to characterize socio-political processes leading to a situation in which different social and political factions can articulate interests and organize themselves. Political change involving a *de facto* authoritarian one-party state would in this framework of analysis denote a change toward a more pluralistic political system. If we take the concept of "political change" to its logical conclusion, it means a very basic alteration of the structures and attitudes of government, both within the present political elite and in the populace.

Realistically speaking, there would seem to be little prospect

[52]

for such a fundamental political change in the ruling structures of the GDR as presently constituted. The SED leadership exercises such tight control over GDR society that such a thoroughgoing political transformation of the system seems out of the question, for the present at least.

On the other hand, we must not be overly pessimistic in this regard. If we project the present processes of increased upward social mobility (the "career society" motivations inculcated in society), plus the trends of present economic expansion, we can see certain long-range prospects for gradual, evolutionary changes *in* (not of) the system. If this is a valid assumption, we should consider the "vulnerability zones" of the party's power, that is, how closely it *must* or *can* control the processes it set in motion during most of the 1960s. Put another way, how far should the dictates of efficiency intrude upon purely political-power considerations of preserving the present system of government?

More specific questions also arise in this context. For example, within the Politburo proper, what policies advocated by representatives of the party's technical experts should be accepted, albeit grudgingly, by its dogmatist members, and to what extent? Also, to what degree should the "experts" in the Politburo accommodate to the policies formulated by those representing the dogmatic strains? As far as we can determine, the "specialist" wing in the Politburo has not been able to attain unquestioned preeminence, largely because of Ulbricht's tactical ability. On the other hand, this wing is influential to the degree that a consensus now prevails in the SED's ruling body that any further change in the system must not be at the high political cost of widespread terror.

Major problems in both foreign and domestic policy face the leadership. In foreign policy they are: political and economic pressures from the Soviet Union, the continuing effects of communist polycentrism, and the influence, basically psychological, of the FRG. The problems rooted in the GDR domestic situation are even more complicated. The two sets of factors influence each other.

Sources of Political Instability

As we have already asserted, the *political* system of the GDR has remained unstable. We can adduce a variety of reasons to substantiate this line of argument.

[53]

First and foremost, substantial segments of the population continue to withhold unqualified, active support from the party and its policies. In fact many are still either openly hostile to the SED or totally uninvolved in political matters.

Secondly, there has not been any widespread development of a "national consciousness," of any widely accepted system of social behavioral norms, or of the "socialist" style of life propounded by the party. Therefore, the average citizen remains insecure in his conceptions of "correct" everyday political behavior — though one must concede that the overall atmosphere in this respect is now far from being as oppressive as it was in 1961 and 1962.

Finally, the GDR remains locked into step with the Soviet Union as far as foreign policy is concerned. Only in recent years, moreover, has it achieved a certain autonomy in matters of domestic policy.

We shall now go into these arguments in more detail. Put briefly, it is our thesis that the present situation in the GDR is one of political instability combined with some degree of socio-economic stability. One of the most important factors in the tendency toward socio-economic stability has been the development of the concept of a "career society." For the people to regard careers in society as offering promise for the future, there must first of all be a basic confidence in the country and society in which these careers are to be pursued. This confidence is necessarily related to the "dependability" or "predictability" of the standards and criteria for occupational and social advancement established by the state or the party. Ample reason for such confidence evidently exists today for hundreds of thousands of ambitious working people in the GDR.

However, when one turns to the political scene, one finds confidence in the political rulers and in the basic precepts of the system in general sorely lacking. This is true even for many of those who represent political power. It is not without good reason that the "independence" or "autonomy" of the GDR are monotonously paraded at every opportunity. One gets the impression that this continuous self-assertion is rooted in deep feelings of insecurity and anxiety. Ulbricht's patent political dependence on the USSR has helped both to create and to reinforce this impression; the close identification of SED Politburo policies with the course of the Soviet Union has, in the twenty

[54]

years since the founding of the GDR, only gradually given way to a somewhat more independent policy, and really only in domestic matters. There are good reasons for this. As has already been pointed out, Ulbricht and the other political leaders know that their close identification with the Soviet Union represents their only chance to assume a relatively important position in the Eastern Bloc, and to a certain degree in European politics as well. They know that this international position can only be consolidated if the GDR proves itself an especially reliable partner of the Soviet Union. A concurrent disadvantage of this policy is, however, a heavy political and economic dependence on the Soviets. Psychologically, this dependency has had a double effect: on the one hand, the SED leadership follows the directives of Moscow or at least waits until the positions adopted by the Kremlin are clear, when it usually adopts them itself with no prompting. On the other hand, the people do not consider the GDR a sovereign state because they feel the result of this dependency deeply. In the light of these psychological and political considerations, the GDR can hardly be considered a sovereign state. In the GDR we find no "national" consciousness in the traditional sense of the term.

The Struggle against Revisionism

A further factor influencing both domestic and foreign policy is the SED leadership's phobia against any type of revisionism. The men in power define the term "revisionism" as standing for any type of thinking having to do with political and social change which does not originate within the SED leadership itself. Ulbricht, in particular, fears the discussion of ideological principles — insofar as he cannot initiate and control such debate himself. This is, on the one hand, a reflection of the authoritarian ruling style of the SED's First Secretary. On the other hand, however, the phenomenon has roots in the history of the KPD and the SED.

In his career Ulbricht has always made prominent individuals in the party scapegoats for political deviations. As early as in the forties and fifties, discussion of political principles had resulted in conflict among SED factions. In the period from 1954 to 1958, Zaisser and Herrnstadt, Schirdewan, Wollweber and Oelssner, and even the political utopian, Harich, were eliminated in such struggles. Some discussion of principle is permitted, but the ultimate verdict is rendered solely by Ulbricht. This was true, for example, in the case of a series of practical suggestions for the reorganization of the economic system which had been formulated as early as 1956–1957 by such "revisionist" economists as Professor Fritz Behrens, one of the outstanding men in this field in the GDR. At that time, Behrens had called for the greater autonomy of enterprises and the delegation of day-to-day economic decision-making to subordinate bodies — thus proving himself to be a precurser of the Liberman reforms in the USSR in the mid 1960s. His suggestions were rejected by the party leadership as "revisionist" and were dismissed without any serious discussion. A few years later, at a time which was politically far more auspicious, Ulbricht adopted Behrens' suggestions and in part implemented them. Therefore, the complex history of East German revisionism must be considered whenever one speaks of politically or ideologically deviant thought in that country, as must all the nuances and connotations which the word "revisionism" has in communist usage.

The rejection of revisionist thinking extends to all segments of the leading groups of the SED, though for different motives. Ulbricht and the conservative party leaders have committed themselves ideologically so strongly that they can not accept or even discuss a clearly deviant political or ideological line. Thus, they sift out and attack all conceptions which deviate from the existing official line. Even younger, ideologically more flexible party leaders, the specialists, managers, and technocrats, have a deep aversion to ideological revisionism, at least in its traditional forms. These men have always seen themselves mainly as pragmatic reformers of the system. They are filled with a deep mistrust of the literary representatives of utopian revisionism, who often had few misgivings about supporting Stalinism. Actually, Stalinism and the literary variants of utopian revisionism were worlds apart. However, in their abstract-dogmatic and totalitarian features, and in their styles of viewing the world and its problems, they were similar. The long-time giants among revisionists — Georg Lukács, Ernst Bloch, Robert Havemann, even their most famous representative in the younger generation, Wolfgang Harich — for a time had, each in his own way, supported Stalinism ideologically — and morally as well, in the eyes of the critical generation of technocrats. The abstract utopias of humanistic socialism had apparently been compatible with a political maneuverability. The critical younger party leaders would probably be more attracted by such authors as Christa Wolf, whose marxistic "morality" would seem more honest intellectually.

However, the younger specialists in the party, like Günter Mittag, reject utopian revisionism in its classical definition for other reasons as well. They do not feel that abstract philosophical theorems about the nature of man and society can be translated into forward-looking policies in this day and age. The political theories of representatives of this utopian thinking — such as Wolfgang Harich's "Platform" — are lacking in concreteness and in political judgment about the potentials and limitations of political action. Thus, to men like Mittag, demands made in 1956 for the abolition of the National People's Army and for the "liberalization of the SED" betray a lack of sensitivity to the political realities of the GDR. The younger specialists realize that in general there is in East Germany a weariness with ideological slogans. For the "new men" in the party the real questions involve concrete, incremental improvements, such as decentralization of the decision-making process and a more direct participation in the economic process on the part of all those involved. On the whole, however, it is not likely that the younger groups will fight "revisionism" in the way the dogmatists have done and — given an appropriate situation — would presumably do again.

These considerations lead us to ask whether, at present or in the foreseeable future, there is any chance for revisionist thinking in the GDR at all. In the context of our analysis we would briefly answer this question as follows: the major goals of the party's leadership in foreign policy — attainment of wide international recognition plus a continuing close relationship with the Soviet Union — are by now so firmly established that they can hardly be questioned, even in the context of discussions which would officially be labelled "revisionist." The same holds true for some basic issues of domestic policy.

However, revisionist approaches still exist, in ideology, literature, the philosophy of arts, and so on. If they gained a certain prominence, they would probably be fought by the party leaders in the traditional way. On the other hand, a new kind of revisionism is emerging, to which the party leadership reacts in a different way, thus widening the range of intra-party discussion.

[57]

The Potentials of and Limitations on Intra-Party Discussion

In line with this new development, the views of one of the most important intellectual pioneers of the "new economic system" should be mentioned briefly. The "case" of Uwe-Jens Heuer demonstrates very clearly the possibilities which exist for a discussion of basic principles in the GDR of today. Heuer (born in 1933), a convinced marxist, is a professor of law. He taught originally at Humboldt University in East Berlin. Since 1967 he has been one of the leading minds in the Central Committee's Central Institute for Socialist Economic Management, established in 1966. Using the concepts of cybernetic systems analysis and information theory, Heuer is trying to interpret his society, the party, and state in their terms. Although on the verge of "revisionist" thinking, his analysis is more differentiated and seems to be more convincing to SED leaders.[47] Heuer's models are highly theoretical, almost completely disregarding the substance of political and ideological reality in GDR society. He is primarily interested in analyzing that society in terms of feed-back processes, or of the effect of information emanating from the entire system and its reaction to various parts of that system. The cybernetic concepts of "self-organization" and "self-regulation" are the central part of his analysis. If subsystems are to react flexibly to the requirements of the entire system, the tasks of the subsystem must be clearly delineated and tightly limited. These tasks must not, however, be planned in detail prematurely, or else the ability of the subsystem to react flexibly will be impaired. In programming, an "institutionally" (organizationally) guaranteed opportunity for the subsystem, e.g., among others the party, to manage its own problems is presumed in order to provide enough latitude for creativity, or "creative learning," as Karl W. Deutsch has termed it. Heuer designates the "material interest" of the individual as the "inner motor" of self-organization — here Heuer is thinking mainly of industrial enterprises. Basing his argument on economic theories, Heuer consistently goes on to demand the application of the principle of self-organization to the entire society. In the final analysis, the concept of self-organization in mainly economic activity logically leads to individual decision on the part of the worker. In order to achieve this, a clear delineation of the relationship between central planning and individual decisions is necessary.

[58]

Heuer views the concept of individual decision as a key in the new formulation of the concept of democracy in the GDR.

The potential political consequences of the cybernetic interpretation of a socialist society can be drawn from what we have already outlined. Heuer's concept taken to its logical conclusion amounts to a limitation on the power of the supreme political body, the Politburo, a power which has up to now been only barely limited. In particular, Heuer's model excludes irrational decisions in the Politburo, such as, for example, decisions whose consequences are relevant for the entire society, but which are taken only as a result of SED factional struggles. A further consequence of this type of thinking is a concentration on the situation exclusively *within* the GDR. The Federal Republic of Germany is no longer considered a significant factor which can disturb the domestic development of GDR society.

Because of such postulates Heuer of necessity came into conflict with official doctrine.[48] The vast decentralization of the system which Heuer demanded appeared politically almost suicidal. His interpretation of reaction processes within society also directly contravened prevailing doctrine, since the SED leadership desperately needed the FRG in the scarecrow role in order to be able to "justify" the more glaring failures of its own policies.

It is worth noting that Heuer was both supported and attacked in the state-controlled press. And though it is true that in 1967 he lost his post as director of the seminar on public law at Humboldt University, he was nonetheless immediately appointed division head for socialist economic law at the Central Institute for Socialist Economic Management. This change meant that students would no longer be exposed to his influence. His publications, as well, were probably subjected to censorship. Under the watchful eye of the SED and to a certain extent isolated, Heuer can, however, still develop his own ideas further.

The Heuer case is interesting insofar as it illustrates the political implications of being deemed "revisionist" by the party. On the one hand, the SED leadership rejects all forms of ideological deviation. Indeed, all revisionist discussion is *a priori* dismissed by the SED, since it might reveal basic flaws in the system of government. On the other hand, those aspects of revisionist thought which can be presented as concepts which reform the society in directions considered desirable have on

[59]

occasion subsequently been adopted by the party. This tactic, of utilizing revisionism to modernize the society, has since 1963–1964 been a hallmark of the party's policy, as developed by the top leadership.

Current Relations with the Federal Republic

As we have already indicated, the attitude of the SED leadership toward the FRG is a ramification of the lack of political stability or real political change in the GDR. In contrast to Heuer, the typical attitude of most leading SED functionaries toward the FRG is one of love-hate. The policies and the world-wide influence (political as well as economic) of the FRG are perceived as overwhelming. The attitude of the political leadership in the SED toward the FRG is thus certainly far more complicated than that of large segments of the GDR population. (The attitude of the normal citizen toward the problem of the "German question" is, however, complicated enough in itself.) For a long period the mere existence of the Federal Republic was seen as a threat to the existence of the GDR. Even today, high SED functionaries still fear that the Soviet Union could one day reach a bilateral settlement with the government of West Germany from which the SED would be excluded. Such a possibility seemed, for example, to be in the offing in the summer of 1964, on the occasion of Adzhubei's visit to West Germany. For this reason, the most important SED political decisions always take into direct account the politics and policies of the FRG.

The primary policy goal of the SED's leadership is the formal recognition of East Germany by the Federal Republic. In order to do so without domestic political upset, the SED has used a wide range of insults and various accusations of militarism and nazism, etc. This judgment is even more clearly substantiated if one considers the views of the FRG which is officially advanced in the GDR. The propagandists of the party have developed an "image" of the FRG, which they propagate, not without success, in the GDR, and also in part in the FRG and especially in selected foreign countries. This image is based on a simplistic, exaggerated contrast: here socialism — there capitalism. The "capitalistic" Federal Republic is "fascist," "revanchist," "militaristic." It has not undergone a thorough denazification. On the contrary, numerous former national socialists are once again in power in the FRG. Moreover, in the FRG an attempt is purportedly being made artificially to preserve obsolete social structures. In an era of increasing social equality, the FRG is still the incarnation of the traditional capitalist class-society. These characteristics are, the argument runs, cleverly disguised by certain processes of modernization.

Within the GDR as well as in foreign countries the propagandists of the SED have tried to peddle the idea that the Federal Republic is the successor of the Third Reich and that the GDR has no connections with previous German history — not only that of the Hitler era but also of the last century. On the other hand, the SED flatly claims a monopoly on certain names and certain events in German history and asserts that they are the basis of its own political and cultural heritage. The political motives for this are easily understood. In the vacuum created after 1945, Germans in both the East and West tried to create a new picture of German history which could in some sense be accepted as positive.

There is a problem, however: how can the SED leadership free itself from the shadow of its powerful, politically recognized sibling to the West? Seen from the GDR's perspective, this can only be accomplished by a policy of abrupt disassociation and complete rejection. This attitude implies the demand for unconditional political recognition of the GDR as a sovereign and separate German state. The SED leadership cannot accept counterdemands from the FRG for self-determination for the whole German people which have been made the precondition for reunification. Therefore, the SED (rhetorically) rejects reunification. On the other hand, the SED leaders realize that the West German government, in particular under the Grand Coalition since the end of 1966 and the SPD-FDR coalition since 1969, is gradually disassociating itself from a policy of isolating the GDR within the Eastern Bloc and from the so-called Hallstein doctrine, which claims that diplomatic relations between the FRG and states that recognize the GDR are in international law incompatible with the FRG's right to sole representation of the German people (*Alleinvertretungsrecht*). The West German government's moves toward relaxation of the strained relations between the two Germanies have become clear in its cautious overtures to Rumania and Czechoslovakia. They are

[61]

also evident in its recent initiatives vis à vis Yugoslavia, diplomatic relations with which had in 1957 been broken off in application of the "Hallstein doctrine." In addition, it had by the fall of 1969 become clear how little the Hallstein doctrine was still being applied in its earlier rigid form. The FRG's reactions to the political recognition of the GDR by Iraq (April 30, 1969), Cambodia (May 8, 1969), the Sudan (May 27, 1969), Syria (June 5, 1969), South Yemen (June 30, 1969), and Egypt (July 11, 1969) are examples of this development. The Bonn administration announced that such recognition was an "unfriendly act" toward the FRG and cancelled economic aid. In South Yemen it shut down its embassy; the same measure was applied in Cambodia. Although these FRG reactions might be called "strong," they were different in nuance from the earlier reactions in the Yugoslav case.

An increased inflexibility in the attitude of the SED — not only in policies relating to the German question but also in domestic policy — went hand in hand with the new West German political efforts vis à vis Eastern Europe, i.e., the so-called *Ostpolitik* of the West German administrations since 1966. It would be wrong, however, to try to construe a direct causal connection between the two. Growing efforts to achieve a moderate degree of autonomy in Eastern Europe, and the further strengthening of polycentristic tendencies in the world communist movement have also influenced the attitude of the SED leadership. Finally, the dynamics of the industrial society in the GDR must once again perforce be mentioned. The party is trying to maintain control over these forces. Thus nothing really basic has changed in the attitude of the SED leadership toward the Federal Republic. This became clear on the occasion of the first meetings between top representatives of both states at Erfurt (March 19, 1970) and Kassel (May 21, 1970).

Relations between the SED and the FRG are also entangled with SED/KPD-SPD relationships, which have been strained for decades. Historically this can be traced to the 1920s and 1930s, which were characterized by deep hatred between the KPD and the Social Democratic Party (SPD). Many members of both parties have still not forgotten that at the end of the twenties Stalin had characterized German Social Democracy as the "twin brother of Fascism." Influential Communist Party politicians in the Weimar Republic had adopted this slogan. In

[62]

addition, personal feuds and unforgotten enmities continue to exist. Herbert Wehner, the SPD's chairman in the Bundestag, had, for example, worked as Walter Ulbricht's secretary in Berlin in the early thirties. He left the KPD during the war. After 1945 there were frequent changes in party allegiance from the Communist to the Social Democratic Party.

In spite of such opposition and such inhibiting factors, in the spring and summer of 1966 the SPD leadership attempted to organize an exchange of public speakers with the SED; the major facets of the German question were to be publically discussed in the GDR as well as in the FRG. After at first accepting this idea, the Politburo of the SED rejected it in June 1966. The actual reasons for this decision have not yet become clear but it is by no means certain that the Soviet had vetoed this exchange. It is, however, quite obvious that Ulbricht feared that the people of the GDR would show overwhelming approval for West German politicians, in particular for Willy Brandt. In addition, it has become public knowledge that even certain members of the SED were not "dependable" enough in their dedication to the SED's political line to be able to meet the challenge of open debate with SPD speakers. Ulbricht did not want to expose the party even remotely to the threat of a political defeat.

The entrance of the SPD into the Grand Coalition at the end of 1966 gave the SED a welcome opportunity to formulate official reasons for the rejection of the exchange. The arguments expressed then, which seemed to preclude any growing accommodation between the SED and the SPD, have been repeated in variations since then.

Today, with the SPD in the governing position, it is much more difficult to decline the offer to relax tensions between the two German states. However, the most important problem for the SED was and remains the SPD's refusal to recognize the GDR. Every opportunity is taken to demand recognition. The SED confronts the SPD leadership with its own program, in which the SPD has stated it wants to follow a "policy of small steps," of "dialogue" with the other Germany. This policy — so it is argued in East Berlin — would inevitably lead to FRG political recognition of the GDR. But since this conclusion is not yet fully accepted by the government of the FRG, it is concluded in East Berlin that the SPD has to kow-tow to the opponents of recognition at all costs in order to remain in power.

[63]

Summary

The political, sociological, and psychological reasons for the lack of meaningful political change in the GDR are, as we have seen, many-sided. The most important points will now be recapitulated. In the first place, one should mention the view of the SED leadership that the GDR is only useful to the Soviet Union as an efficient and — at least in the socio-economic sense — stable system; that the major political goal of the GDR, which is, together with the Soviet Union, to play the dominant role in the Warsaw Pact and COMECON, can only be pursued if the prerequisite — a functional, dynamic, economic system — has been fulfilled. From the standpoint of the SED leadership, political change would jeopardize existing socio-economic stability. In this, the SED leadership gets at least indirect support from parts of the populace which are also — albeit for different reasons — interested in the socio-economic stability of the system.

One should also mention the psychological side of the problem. For the older generation of SED leaders, political concepts such as "pluralism of forces," "political change," etc., and their content are fundamentally suspect. All their lives these men have believed that the "class enemy exploits the people" under the guise of these concepts. The SED leadership also fears — especially since the summer crisis of 1968 in Czechoslovakia — that control of their system could slip from their hands if currents of real political change were initiated in even one segment of society. Finally, Ulbricht fears that the FRG could capitalize politically on any relaxation in the GDR. For this reason, he sees the only way to relieve the tension of the German question and of Central and Eastern Europe to be in the gradual consolidation of the domestic and foreign position of the GDR. Apparently, his rationale is that such consolidation will sooner or later bring political recognition to the GDR, including political recognition from the Federal Republic.

Because of these reasons, which result from the GDR's domestic and international situation, the SED is strongly opposed to any kind of political change (as defined here), thus proving the GDR's political instability as well as limiting the range of the system's modernization.

IV

THE POSITION OF THE GDR
IN THE EAST EUROPEAN PACT SYSTEM

Both the Warsaw Pact and COMECON are primarily in-
struments to enforce and protect the Soviet Union's hegemonial
claims in Eastern Europe. This was reconfirmed by the inter-
vention in Czechoslovakia in the summer of 1968. The claims of
the Soviet Union to hegemony are manifold and are of a political,
military, economic, and ideological nature.

The GDR and the Warsaw Pact

In 1955 the Warsaw Pact was signed by the Soviet Union
and the other Eastern Bloc nations as a multilateral military
assistance pact. The participating states have always maintained
that it was the admission of the FRG into NATO in May 1955
which precipitated the formation of the Warsaw Pact. In reality,
the Warsaw Pact supplements both the bilateral military assistance agreements the Soviet Union had in the 1940s concluded
with several Eastern Bloc countries and the individual assistance
agreements the nations of the Eastern Bloc already had with each
other. Finally, in 1956–1957, the Soviet Union concluded additional bilateral military assistance pacts with most of the
members of the Warsaw Pact. An additional agreement with the
GDR was signed in the spring of 1957.

Though the Warsaw Pact had gone into effect in mid-1955,
the GDR was only accepted as a full member at the beginning
of 1956. It is fully represented on the Political Consultative
Committee as well as on its auxiliary committees, on the Permanent Commission, and in the Joint Secretariat. Since the
middle of 1956, the GDR Minister for National Defense (at the
time of writing, Army General Karl-Heinz Hoffman) has occupied the post of one of the First Deputy Supreme Commanders
of the Warsaw Pact forces. The Supreme Commander has always
been a Soviet marshal.

The formal structure of the Warsaw Pact has changed very little over the years. One important development, however, is that the relative stature of the GDR's National People's Army changed in 1956. Since then, the armed forces of the GDR have been members of the "first strategic squadron," which is composed of particularly dependable and effective troops. About 75 per cent of the officers of the NVA are presently members of the SED. Comparably high percentages hold among non-commissioned officers and enlisted men. The Soviets seem to value the political dependability of at least large segments of the NVA even more than they do their military importance. On the other hand troops of the other Pact nations are in all likelihood considered less dependable by the Soviets.

In this context it should, however, also be mentioned that the GDR has been considerably handicapped by its membership in the Warsaw Pact. In the first place, unlike the situation for other member nations, all of the GDR's forces are under the control of the Supreme Command of the Warsaw Pact. By the end of 1969 they must have come to some 200,000 men under arms. Furthermore, in the event of war, the GDR cannot decide for itself what kind of assistance it will give, this right having been given to the other member nations. The GDR is also further handicapped by the additional agreement which it made with the Soviet Union in 1957, according to which Soviet troop commanders have the right to conduct military maneuvers with their own army in the GDR *without* the previous consent of the GDR government. The Soviet Union has at various times had from 250,000 to 400,000 Red Army soldiers permanently stationed in the GDR. In the event that their security is threatened, the Soviet commanders can at their own discretion declare a state of martial law. No official explanation for such clauses of agreement has ever been made.

The GDR and COMECON

In 1950 the GDR joined the Council for Mutual Economic Aid (COMECON), which had been founded in 1949. From the beginning, the GDR has been fully represented on all the organization's supreme bodies: the Council's Meeting, the Conference of the National Representatives, the Permanent Commissions, and the Executive Committee (established in 1962), as well as on the International Bank for Trade and Cooperation, which has had its headquarters in Moscow since 1964. Of the twenty-two permanent commissions which exist today, three have headquarters in East Berlin (i.e., those for the chemical industry, construction machinery, and standardization of industrial equipment). The Executive Committee is located in Moscow. The meetings of the Council are rotated among the capital cities of the member nations. Of the twenty-two meetings held up to December 1969, three were in East Berlin, among them the XXII Meeting of January 21–23, 1969, at which the twentieth anniversary of COMECON was celebrated.

While, in what we have chosen to call the "first stage," from 1950 to 1961, the formal status of the GDR in COMECON was not very high, its relative position improved considerably during the "second stage." Three fundamental causes may be cited for this improvement: 1/ the economic situation in the GDR, which had stabilized since the construction of the Wall and the introduction of the "new economic system"; 2/ the observance of the "basic principles of international socialist division of labor," which were the subject of a resolution adopted at the XVI COMECON meeting in 1967. The SED economic planners have since complied very conscientiously with the Council's demand (i.e., it was not a recommendation) for further specialization and less autarchy. Production, especially in the key industries — the chemical, electrotechnical and electronic industries, heavy machinery construction, and the precision-tool and optical industries — has been based on the arrangements made in COMECON meetings. Finally, mention should in this connection be made of the Sino-Soviet conflict, which in the eyes of many observers made the Soviet Union more dependent on its European allies, in particular on the GDR.

The GDR has clearly strengthened its position further in the third phase of participation in COMECON, since 1965–1966. In addition to a general upswing in economic production, further specialization in important branches of industry, which has proved more successful in the GDR than in other Eastern Bloc countries, and the increased degree of automatization, might be cited as the chief factors responsible for this development. Thus, for one thing, the GDR's assigned role in COMECON places limits on its contribution to key industrial products. However, by exporting certain products, the GDR has achieved an economic monopoly in Eastern Europe — especially in the chem-

[67]

ical industry. The economic policy of the GDR is, therefore, in direct contrast to the more "universalistic" concept of the Rumanians, who want to develop their *entire* national economy within the framework of COMECON.

Political Aspects of the Economic Significance of the GDR

The Soviet Union is interested in molding a complicated network of bilateral affiliations within COMECON, especially in the economic sphere, because it has a monopoly on certain raw materials and because it often makes "bloc ruble" credit arrangements with COMECON partners for these raw materials. In contrast with leading Hungarian economic planners, who feel overly close cooperation with the Soviet Union within COMECON to be dangerous for East European national economies, the major figures in the GDR Politburo have for years considered the improvement of ties with the Soviet Union and close bilateral cooperation within COMECON as offering the outstanding opportunities for achieving recognition of the GDR as a *bona fide* nation.

In terms of the above goals, the GDR has benefitted greatly from its relatively high production potential, whose use is planned with bilateral arrangements in mind. As is clear from the 1968 growth rates in COMECON trading patterns, this economic potential is being with increasing success transformed into political power within the Bloc. It is for example considered probable that the Soviet-initiated policy which today in some degree obligates all East European countries to slacken their contacts with the FRG may be traced to Ulbricht's influence. Certainly Ulbricht has made explicit to the COMECON partners the desirability of "eliminating alien influences" from the GDR's economy (which has elsewhere been termed "eliminating the attraction of the FRG magnet"). His efforts at isolating Czechoslovakia in the Bloc and, simultaneously, at preventing the isolation of the GDR, have also met with some degree of success. As these policies prove more acceptable and more successful, the political influence of the GDR within COMECON increases. In all this, Ulbricht's overall goal is to see the GDR truly independent of the West in the economic sense and occupying a strong position within the Eastern Bloc, which, hopefully, could — within six to ten years — demonstrate that it could be a self-sufficient "socialist economic system." By that time, Ulbricht

[68]

would hope to have transformed GDR industry into an economically efficient system which would, subject of course to the Soviet veto power, issue all the basic "edicts" to the COMECON nations.

This combination of economic and political power and their application have since the summer of 1968 tended to work in the GDR's favor. The functional reorganizations of the economy within the "new economic system" — and the present phase of development which is called the "economic system of socialism" — are today officially recognized by the Soviets. The increasing number of technologically important inventions in the GDR contributes further to the prestige of the country. The "GDR model," the concept of a dynamic, bureaucratically centralized economic and social system, has also found the political approval of the Soviets. This is in contrast with the Soviet reaction against both the nationalist but conservative conception of the Rumanians and the national and "liberal" plans in Czechoslovakia. This pragmatic, efficiency-oriented outlook, which, as we have seen, must not automatically be equated with "liberal" trends in the political sphere, has not only been approved by the Soviets, it is even being copied. For this reason, the *Proposals of the GDR Concerning the United Socialist Economic Association*, a report which Ulbricht delivered to the ninth plenum of the Central Committee of the SED in 1968, are of particular significance for the future organization of COMECON. Once again Ulbricht proposed a tightening of planning and an acceleration in the extension of the right of the COMECON nations to conclude international economic agreements.[49]

In concluding, we should note that naturally the policies of the SED are beclouded by the partition of Germany. Ulbricht knows that a prime alternative for Soviet foreign policy has always been cooperation with the FRG. Such an arrangement could only come about at the expense of the GDR. Ulbricht's long-range policy is therefore also aimed toward edging the FRG away from its role as a potential future partner of the Soviet Union.

Economic Cooperation Between the Soviet Union and the GDR

Since the conclusion of the Treaty of Friendship, Mutual Assistance and Cooperation between the USSR and the GDR in June 1964, political, economic, scientific, and technical ties between the two countries have been further expanded. The long-term trade agreement of December 1965 is particularly significant in this respect. Operative until 1970, it provides for a total export volume of 60 billion East marks (i.e., some 15 billion dollars). Several specific clauses of this trade agreement between the GDR and the USSR are, as we shall explain below, of special interest because they form the background for the growing political and economic significance of the GDR within COMECON. The same holds — perhaps to an even greater degree — for scientific and technical cooperation between the two countries.

The Soviet Union, which in 1968 took perhaps 42 per cent of the GDR's total trade, is East Germany's foremost trade partner. With about 18 per cent of the export trade of the Soviet Union, the GDR also occupies the position of the Soviet Union's leading trade partner.[50] The GDR imports the following raw materials from the USSR, the percentage in parentheses indicating the percentage of total import of the particular raw material in 1967: anthracite (57.8); iron products (81.9); petroleum (88.0); and wool and cotton (90.3). In addition, the GDR also imported non-ferrous metals, heating oil, wood fibre, and paper pulp from the Soviet Union. Since 1967–1968, however, the percentages of semi-finished products and components for computer equipment and of other sophisticated machinery have increased considerably. These imports are composed primarily of wire rod and sheet steel, but they also include semiconductor devices and radio tubes as well as railroad passenger cars, trucks, and tractors. While in 1968 raw materials still composed 60 per cent of all GDR imports from the USSR and foodstuffs, 20 per cent, imports of semi-manufactured and manufactured products from the Soviet Union were already at about 20 per cent. This figure will probably increase considerably in 1970, to some 30 per cent. These figures reflect changes in the economic ties between the two countries. These changes make the GDR more a "junior partner" of the USSR than a country in abject economic subservience to it.

Import statistics for the USSR show that the GDR has in many areas achieved a position of monopoly as the basic "supplier" partner. The Soviet Union in 1966 took about 27 per cent of its total machinery and equipment imports from the GDR. In certain branches of industry, figures which go back as far as

[70]

1965 are considerably higher.[51] Thus, at that time, the Soviet Union imported 80 per cent of its metallurgical equipment, 75 per cent of its marine diesel motors, 73 per cent of its dredging and road-making equipment, and 52 per cent of its railroad passenger cars from the GDR.

In conclusion, projected delivery of raw materials from the Soviet Union to the individual COMECON nations, from 1966 to 1970, further confirms the favored position of the GDR. (See Table 6.)

Table 6

PROJECTED RAW MATERIAL EXPORTS FROM THE SOVIET UNION
TO COMECON NATIONS
1966–1970

EXPORTED COMMODITIES	BULGARIA	HUNGARY	GDR	POLAND	CZECHOSLO-VAKIA
Petroleum (in millions of tons)	15.7	16.0	36.0	26.0	39.0
Hard coal (in millions of tons)	21.0	4.6	31.5	—	19.0
Cotton (in thousands of tons)	190.0	195.0	410.5	415.0	300.0

Source: *Mezhdunarodnaia zhizn'*, vol. 10/1967, p. 41.

The cooperation between the GDR and the USSR, which has become more like a partnership, becomes particularly clear if the bilateral Governmental Commission for Economic, Scientific, and Technical Cooperation (founded in 1966) is brought into our analysis. The fifth meeting of this Commission took place in Moscow in December 1968. On the basis of agreements worked out by the Commission, long-range contracts (thru 1975) have been entered into concerning specialization and cooperation in areas crucial to the GDR's economy — such as the chemical industry, electronics, nuclear engineering, the manufacture of scientific equipment, and certain branches of machine-tool manufacture. In addition, the Commission has also established some thirty groups of experts, which are responsible for bilateral contacts between the following GDR ministries and their counterparts in the Soviet Union: the ministries for Electrical Engineering and Electronics, Light Industry, Mining,

[71]

Metallurgy and Potash, Transportation, for the Food Industry and for *Bezirk*-led Industries, and for Health. There are also bilateral consultations for the electric power industry and for standardization of special equipment for the smelting industry, for machine manufacturing, and in the chemical, cellulose, and paper industries. Finally, there is close cooperation between numerous scientific research institutes in the universities, higher technical schools, academies, ministries, and industrial combines in both countries.

The GDR vis à vis Other COMECON Countries

Even if both economic connections and export balances between the Soviet Union and the GDR underscore the latter's "special relation" with the USSR in comparison with all other COMECON countries, East German exports to the major countries of Eastern Europe have increased in parallel fashion since 1960. (See Table 7.)

Table 7

TOTAL EXPORTS FROM THE
GDR TO EASTERN EUROPE
1960–1968

| EXPORT TO: | 1960 | 1967 | 1968 | 1967 |
	(IN MILLIONS OF MARKS)			(1960-100)
Bulgaria	289.9	525.2	636.6	181.2
Czechoslovakia	806.8	1,328.1	1,689.4	164.6
Hungary	395.8	770.5	812.7	194.7
Poland	772.6	1,195.2	1,224.1	154.7
Rumania	202.9	377.6	376.1	186.1
Yugoslavia	143.8	272.7	318.3	189.6

Source: *Statistisches Jahrbuch 1968 der Deutschen Demokratischen Republik*, p. 374; *Statistisches Jahrbuch 1969*, p. 298.

Although the overall increase in the rate of exports to the COMECON countries was greater than increase in exports to the Soviet Union, which increased to 152 per cent in 1967 taking 1960 as our base, the absolute monetary value of exports from East Germany to the Soviet Union is considerably higher than that of goods which were exported to all the other COMECON countries combined, in a ratio of 5.9 billion marks as against 4.2 billion in 1967.

Examining total GDR imports from the most important countries in Eastern Europe between 1960 and 1967, we find that there were in part higher but, on the whole, lower increase rates for imports than for exports. A higher increase rate for imports is particularly clear in the case of Bulgaria, which, for the most part, exports raw materials and agricultural products in return for its imports from the GDR. (See Table 8.)

Table 8

TOTAL IMPORTS OF THE GDR
FROM EASTERN EUROPE
1960–1968

IMPORTED FROM	1960	1967	1968	1967
	(IN MILLION OF MARKS)			(1960-100)
Bulgaria	229.6	480.3	513.8	209.2
Czechoslovakia	785.2	1,335.8	1,380.9	170.1
Hungary	392.5	643.7	720.3	164.0
Poland	457.0	692.0	942.4	151.4
Rumania	218.2	297.4	324.4	136.3
Yugoslavia	185.6	279.2	242.1	150.4

Source: Statistisches Jahrbuch 1968 der Deutschen Demokratischen Republik, p. 375; Statistisches Jahrbuch 1969, p. 299.

In 1967, the GDR imported from the Soviet Union some 5.95 billion marks worth of goods (an increase of 148 per cent in terms of the 1960 turnover).

In addition to the GDR's foreign trade with the USSR, the volume of GDR goods traded with Czechoslovakia exceeds the total GDR trade with other COMECON countries. Of course, Czechoslovakia is the only COMECON country with the exception of the USSR which is equipped to supply the GDR with a wide range of special goods, which would otherwise have to be obtained from the West. In 1967, total exchange between the two countries represented 9.5 per cent of the total foreign trade of the GDR (i.e., the equivalent in approximate terms of the volume of trade with the FRG). The close East German economic ties with Czechoslovakia have not changed essentially since the summer of 1968. After the USSR and the GDR, Czechoslovakia has the third strongest industrial potential in the Eastern Bloc. Only a few years after the GDR, this country also entered a phase of economic "intensification," i.e., specialization. "Intensifica-

[73]

tion" means an increase in the rationalization of investments as opposed to new investments, a raising of technical standards, improvements in labor productivity, and greater cooperation among major enterprises.

In accordance with the COMECON agreements, inter-industrial cooperation has been extended beyond national boundaries, but only within the socialist world. Especially in the case of countries with somewhat analogous economic structures, such as the GDR and Czechoslovakia, we find that the partners have, in particular since 1967, made a series of agreements about "production cooperation" which are equally advantageous to both sides. Thus, for example, GDR enterprises specializing in electrical engineering have established direct contacts with comparable enterprises in the CSSR. A "division of labor" in the production of industrial goods has been one result of these direct contacts, having been achieved in engine-tool manufacturing, medical technology, in heavy electrical engineering, and in electronics. In addition to this type of production cooperation, agreements have also been made for joint research and development projects. Of Czechoslovakia's total export to the GDR in 1967, the share of products resulting from this division of labor in production came to about 16 per cent.

Press releases which covered the convocation of the Committee for Economic, Technical, and Scientific Cooperation between Hungary and the GDR, which was held in the fall of 1968, show the increasing significance of the GDR's economic ties with Hungary. Foreign trade volume in 1968 rose by 13 per cent over the figure for 1967. In 1969 it in fact exceeded the exchange level projected for 1970. The figures for import and export between both countries have increased greatly, particularly in the following commodities: automobiles and trucks, agricultural machinery, communication engineering products, electronic and X-ray equipment and various optical products. At the conference cited above, it was resolved to form a joint task force which, beginning in 1969, was to concern itself with the differences in the economic management systems of both countries. Of particular note was the suggestion, by Hungary, that this task force enter into a discussion of one of the most enigmatic of the as yet unsolved problems of COMECON as a whole — the problem of a "convertible socialist currency." Such bilateral cooperation between countries which are, in terms of their economic reform, the most progressive countries in the Eastern Bloc, deserves even more attention if one notes that while the Hungarians repeatedly emphasized the strengthening of the national sovereignty of the partner countries, the East Germans continued to stress the urgency of priority for the supranational integration of each individual Eastern Bloc country.

Unresolved Problems

The policy of the USSR and the GDR, which, in spite of all its drawbacks, has on the whole proved successful in bringing the countries of COMECON into closer interdependence has nevertheless run into a series of difficulties of fairly recent vintage. All partner countries have based their current national economic plans upon the directives of COMECON. This "adjustment" has nevertheless not been satisfactory, chiefly because the individual countries have become more differentiated in terms of their social structures and more especially of their economies; since growth rates are not synchronized; and since no uniform right to make economic agreements has been formally codified; and finally, because the problems of foreign trade and contract prices have not as yet been dealt with decisively.

An average growth rate of industrial productions in the COMECON countries was projected as follows for the period 1966–1970. (See Table 9.)

Table 9

AVERAGE ANNUAL INCREASE IN INDUSTRIAL PRODUCTION
IN COMECON COUNTRIES, 1956–1970

(in percentages)

COUNTRIES	1956–1960 ACTUAL INDEX	1961–1965 ACTUAL INDEX	1966–1970 PLANNED INDEX
Bulgaria	15.9	11.7	11.2
Czechoslovakia	10.5	5.2	5.1–5.4
GDR	9.2	6.0	6.5–7.0
Hungary	7.5	7.5	5.0–6.0
Mongolia	18.1	10.5	11.2–12.5
Poland	9.9	8.5	7.5
Rumania	10.9	13.8	10.6–11.6
Soviet Union	10.4	8.6	8.1–8.5

Source: *Deutsche Aussenpolitik*, Berlin (East), 2/1968, p. 225.

[75]

It is clear from Table 9 that — together with Czechoslovakia and Hungary — the GDR will achieve a lower growth rate than other COMECON countries through the period from 1966 to 1970. Thus, like the USA and the FRG, the GDR finds itself in that category of highly industrialized countries whose yearly growth rate no longer exceeds from 4 to 5 per cent. This figure is therefore not exceptional. On the other hand, in the next few years the economic growth-rate gap between the other partner countries and the GDR will diminish still further, so that the leading or predominant position of the GDR is in numerous areas likely to lose its significance. For this reason, it is necessary for the SED leadership to implement quickly those long-term, structurally decisive decisions in the Eastern Bloc which most closely correspond to its own interests.

A further potential problem lies in the fact that the right to make economic agreements has not yet been satisfactorily worked out. This becomes particularly noteworthy when we examine the scientific and technical inventions which are being produced by the GDR at an increasing rate. For many years, they have been made available free of charge to the other COMECON countries. The arguments advanced for this procedure, particularly in Soviet international law, were the "principles of socialist internationalism" and the "principles of mutual socialist aid." The counter-argument has been repeatedly made, especially by economic lawyers in the GDR, that the "scientifictechnical revolution" and the "economic competition between global power systems" require still newer forms of regulation even in contract law. If one accepts this second theory, then the claim can be made that scientific and technical inventions should be considered "commodities." Patent agreements would then be designated "the most expedient form" of regulating the exchange of these "commodities."

The "price clause" of the COMECON is possibly an even more serious issue. After a period of price-freezing from 1950 to 1958, which was admittedly designed to stabilize the "socialist system" and to protect it from the forces and influence of the world market, the COMECON partners agreed on certain principles regarding prices. First of all basic prices were established in terms of prices of goods on the "capitalist" market, at first those of 1957 and later those of 1960–1964. On this basis, prices were established between two COMECON trading partners.

[76]

Such prices are not subject to market fluctuations and should, in theory, remain stable for a long time. In special cases, involving for example the introduction of new products, "standing prices" can be agreed on. This measure has hit the GDR especially hard, since its inventions and technical developments could not be put on the market at going prices.

Since 1965–1966, COMECON prices have more closely approximated world prices, but not to a very impressive degree. Especially because of COMECON isolation from world markets and because of the concept of a "socialistically-determined price," which has nothing to do with world market price and affects only COMECON countries, prices for numerous products and accomplishments in COMECON countries have been and still are higher than world market prices. This has a particularly unfavorable effect on the expanding economy of the GDR, in terms of imports as well as exports, since approximately 22 per cent of the GDR's total foreign trade, with Western and underdeveloped countries, thereby suffers a considerable disadvantage.

The GDR is not, at least directly, exposed to the competition of world markets, and it would not yet be competitive with them for many reasons. In spite of numerous price reforms in the GDR, many prices are not yet realistic. For this reason, foreign trade prices have not yet operated as a dynamic factor in COMECON. But, in order to be able to participate in international worldwide scientific and technical developments, which are reflected in changing prices on the world market, COMECON prices must be more closely adapted to world market prices. For economic and political reasons, such considerations have not yet intruded upon the thinking of the SED leadership. Ulbricht even denounced this variant of "economic revisionism" as recently as October 1968, in his speech at the Ninth Plenum of the SED Central Committee.

Finally, the problem of the international convertibility of the Soviet ruble should be mentioned. In the last few years, several countries, such as Poland, Hungary, and Rumania, have been increasingly adamant in their demand for a convertible "foreign trade ruble" based on gold. Some of these countries had an excess of rubles in their COMECON "bank accounts" in Moscow; other countries (cf. Rumania) have geared themselves to trade with the West. In order to facilitate trade with Western countries and thereby induce desired growth in the Eastern

[77]

European countries, COMECON's Executive Committee in the spring of 1966 resolved to make the ruble internationally convertible; but this resolution has only partially been realized. Such multilateralism has not yet truly replaced bilateralism in COMECON.

For the moment, however, such a policy would be neither in the interest of the Soviet Union nor of the GDR. Long-range plans set the limits of delivery and purchase goods for years in advance, thus facilitating production and marketing planning for industrial products. In addition, the COMECON market, sheltered from international competition, is attractive for relatively high-grade products and equipment from the GDR, which would as yet only occasionally be accepted on the world market. This is all the more true because GDR industry is concentrating on exports to numerous COMECON countries. One reason for this is, of course, the GDR's desire to supplant Czechoslovakian industry which has been disrupted by the "irregularities" of the summer and fall of 1968. In addition, the greater latitude in foreign trade policy which numerous state enterprises now have — at least with partner countries of the Eastern Bloc — is of benefit to the current export "offensive" of the GDR.

CONCLUSIONS

Since 1963, all the indicators of a dynamic, differentiated industrial society have been visible in the GDR. Particular emphasis should be placed on social change, mobility, and social conflicts, terms which are by no means used here to denote necessarily disruptive processes. These signs of differentiation have also infected the SED. Younger party specialists and managers have assumed numerous leadership positions. The operational axiom of functional efficiency in the economy and in East German society has become basic to the preservation of the system, second only to the consolidation of power. The career horizons of individuals and of different social groups have thus been extended by the party itself. For many, life in the GDR has become more worth living, more stimulating.

On the basis of these indications one cannot, however, speak of any true political change in the system. For the SED is and has throughout been the seat of political and social power, which permits social pluralism only as long as its political hegemony is not threatened. Every communist system must grant a certain minimal degree of latitude to the process of creative learning, which an industrial society requires to maintain its dynamism. Party leadership in the GDR has thus far granted little more than this modicum.

Increasing economic stability on the domestic scene is still, as we have seen, accompanied by political instability. Since it may well be difficult for the SED to achieve political stabilization from within itself, the party's foreign policy and its foreign trade determinations are of considerable importance to the domestic situation of the country. The planners of the GDR policy and economy have never sought national independence. On the contrary, they have always regarded a merger with the systems of the Soviet Union and the other Eastern European countries as the optimal means to stabilize the GDR. For many years the economic system of the GDR has been oriented by the SED leadership predominantly toward the Soviet Union and the

COMECON markets. The leadership considers the further integration of the GDR into COMECON as its economic and political as well as its "national" best bet to enhance the country's importance vis à vis the Soviet Union and to approach closer the goal of international political recognition. At least psychologically, this policy has had positive feed-back on the domestic situation since the growing international recognition of the GDR makes many groups proud of "their" country.

However, it is evident that the interests of individual COMECON countries — those which are technically relatively highly developed (cf. Czechoslovakia, Hungary) as well as those which are chiefly agrarian (Rumania) — can hardly be brought into line with the economic and political interests of the GDR in the near future. Until 1975, that is, until the time for which the economic planners in the GDR have predicted "economic consolidation," the COMECON market will still be of such a nature that the GDR will be able to increase its exports and further strengthen its economic and social system. However, on the basis of information available at present, the GDR may in the forseeable future run into difficulties. Such difficulties would result from growing economic and political competition on the part of those COMECON nations which are themselves undergoing important socio-economic changes.

Thus the SED's stubborn pursuit of international recognition for the GDR is highly motivated by pressures resulting from its present political and economic domestic situation as well as from prospective intra-block developments.

FOOTNOTES

1. Norman J. G. Pounds, *Eastern Europe* (Chicago: Aldine Publishing Co., 1969), pp. 280–281.
2. Thus the GDR had the highest annual population loss in the world. See *same*, p. 232. The official West German figures for the refugee movement are published in *A bis Z: Ein Taschen- und Nachschlagebuch über den Anderen Teil Deutschlands*, ed. by the Bundesministerium für gesamtdeutsche Fragen, Bonn, 11th and revised edition (Bonn: Deutscher Bundes-Verlag, 1969), p. 212.
3. *Statistisches Jahrbuch 1969 der Deutschen Demokratischen Republik*, published by the Staatliche Zentralverwaltung für Statistik (Berlin: Staatsverlag der Deutschen Demokratischen Republik, 14th volume, 1969), pp. 444–445. If not otherwise noted, all figures mentioned in this chapter are taken from this edition of the *Statistisches Jahrbuch der DDR*.
4. *Same*, p. 57.
4a. Wilhelm Zaisser, then a member of the Politburo and Minister for State Security, was ousted from the SED in 1954. Together with Rudolf Herrnstadt, then a member of the Politburo and chief editor of the party paper *Neues Deutschland*, Zaisser was accused of "anti-Party factional activity" (in German "parteifeindliche Fraktionsbildung") in 1953. Karl Schirdewan, then the party's Secretary for Organization and Information and a member of the SED Politburo, and Ernst Wollweber, Zaisser's successor as Minister for State Security, were the spokesmen of an anti-Ulbricht opposition in 1958. They too were charged with "factional activity" and lost their party functions. Cf. Carola Stern, *Ulbricht: Eine Politische Biographie* (Köln and Berlin: Kiepenheuer & Witsch, 1963), pp. 165 ff. This study appeared in English translation as *Ulbricht: A Political Biography* (New York: Praeger, 1965).
5. The three types of LPGs differ among each other along the following lines. Type I is characterized by common use of the land "contributed" by its constituents, plus common use of its grazing lands. In Type II all machinery and equipment for tilling the "commonly held" land are socialized. In Type III the total enterprise, including all its inventories (i.e. both "live" and "dead" categories), is socialized. In Types I and II, households are permitted 0.5 hectares of land for their own use, whereas in Type III families may maintain only a small house garden for their own support. Types I and II represent lower stages of socialization and are supposed to merge into Type III in the course of time. In 1968, there were some 11,513 LPGs in all three categories.

6. The *Neue Ökonomische System der Planung und Leitung der Volks-wirtschaft* (*NÖSPL*) was launched in 1963. Cf. the *Richtlinie für das neue ökonomische System der Planung und Leitung der Volkswirt-schaft* of July 11, 1963, published in *Gesetzblatt der DDR*, Part II, No. 64, 1963, pp. 453 ff.

7. Cf. Jean Edward Smith's survey on "private and semi-state firms" in his book, *Germany Beyond the Wall: People, Politics . . . and Prosperity* (Boston & Toronto: Little, Brown and Co., 1969), pp. 101 ff.

8. For further details see Thomas A. Baylis, "The New Economic System: The Role of the Technocrats in the GDR," *Survey* (October 1966), pp. 139 ff.

9. As far as we know, no English translation of the SED's statutes and program is available. An English version of the 1968 Constitution is printed in the appendix to Jean Edward Smith's book, *Germany Beyond the Wall, cited*, pp. 245–272.

10. Constitution of the German Democratic Republic (1968), *same*, p. 246.

11. Cf. Hannah Arendt, *The Origins of Totalitarianism*, 3rd edition, (New York: Harcourt, Brace & Co., 1966); Carl J. Friedrich and Zbigniew K. Brzezinski, *Totalitarian Dictatorship and Autocracy*, 2nd edition, revised by Carl J. Friedrich (Cambridge, Mass.: Harvard University Press, 1965). Also Robert Burrowes' review article on both these books, "Totalitarianism: The Revised Standard Version," vol. 21, no. 2, *World Politics* (January 1969), pp. 272 ff.

12. Since 1967, in their official statements the SED functionaries have replaced "new economic system of planning and management of the people's economy" by "economic system of socialism" — thus indicating that an introductory phase of the new system had been completed. This change has however not yet been decreed.

13. See Dieter Albrecht, "Aussenwirtschaft im ökonomischen System des Sozialismus," vol. 23, no. 9, *Einheit* (1968), p. 1138.

14. According to Hans Müller and Karl Reissig, *Wirtschaftswunder DDR* (Berlin: Dietz Verlag, 1968), p. 475.

15. Cf. in addition to footnote 2, Jean Edward Smith, *Germany Beyond the Wall, cited*, pp. 87–88.

16. *Statistisches Jahrbuch 1969 der DDR, cited*, p. 436.

17. According to Harry Maier, "Probleme des Verhältnisses von Bildung und Wirtschaftswachstum im ökonomischen System des Sozialismus," vol. 16, no. 12, *Wirtschaftswissenschaft* (1968), p. 1956.

18. Cf. Dieter Claessens *et al.*, *Sozialkunde der Bundesrepublik Deutsch-land* (Düsseldorf-Köln: Eugen Diederichs Verlag, 1965), pp. 156 and 165.

19. Hennecke became the first East German "Stakhanovite" and epitomized the SED's attempt to transpose Soviet production incentive techniques (with their stress on "moral" [ideological] rather than "material" [economic] incentives) to the GDR economy. There was a subsequent raising of work norms throughout the economy. Hennecke thus became the inspirational symbol for the "activist" movement of the

late 1940s. This movement, dominated and manipulated by the SED and the FDGB, was aimed at spurring whole groups of workers in the same enterprise to greater productivity. This was to be achieved mainly by raising labor productivity and decreasing production costs.

20. The largest yearly turnover in the *Bezirk* of Leipzig for 1964 was 45 per cent. See Herbert F. Wolf, "Die Fluktuation der Beschäftigten eines Montagebetriebes in soziologischer Sicht," in Günther Bohring and Kurt Braunreuther, eds., *Soziologie und Praxis* (Berlin: Dietz Verlag, 1965), pp. 177 ff.

21. The changing figures for persons under twenty-five who are permanently engaged in agriculture will serve to indicate the exodus of younger people from the countryside to the city. Thus, from 1961 to 1968, this figure fell from 68,876 to 45,504. Although the number of *all* those permanently employed in agricultural work also decreased in this period by a loss of about 10 per cent, the percentage of young people leaving came to nearly 30 per cent. See *Statistisches Jahrbuch 1969 der DDR, cited*, p. 181.

22. Richard Herber and Herbert Jung, *Kaderarbeit im System sozialistischer Führungstätigkeit* (Berlin: Staatsverlag der Deutschen Demokratischen Republik, 1968), p. 267. The authors designated the following as "leading positions": plant managers (*Werkdirektoren*), technical, economic and commercial directors, chief accountants, cadre leaders.

23. Rainer Falke and Hans Modrow, *Auswahl und Entwicklung von Führungskadern* (Berlin: Staatsverlag der Deutschen Demokratischen Republik, 1967), pp. 147 and 204.

24. *Same*, p. 14.

25. Figures on consumption patterns are based on information obtained from the various issues of the *Statistisches Jahrbuch der DDR*. Those figures which were not prepared by the author himself have been taken from an article entitled "Zur Konsumgüterversorgung in Mitteldeutschland seit 1960," worked out by the Deutsches Institut für Wirtschaftsforschung, no. 47, *Wochenbericht* (24 November 1967), pp. 247–250.

25a. Individual consumption of higher-priced foodstuffs increased as follows, as seen in 1960 and 1967 (figures for 1967 given in parentheses): meat, 55 kg (61.4 kg); edible fats (converted according to percentage of fat), 27.4 kg (29.4 kg); fresh vegetables, 48 kg (56.8 kg); tropical and subtropical fruit, 7.1 kg (11.1 kg); and eggs, 197 (216).

25b. Individual consumption of expensive luxury items increased as follows, as seen in 1960 and 1967 (figures for 1967 given in parentheses): roasted coffee beans, 1.1 kg (1.9 kg); alcoholic drinks, 3.5 liters (5.3 liters); beer, 79.5 liters (84.5 liters); wine and champagne, 3.2 liters (4.7 liters); and cigarettes, 1,069 (1,150).

26. Durable goods for each 100 households, in 1960 and 1967 (with figures for 1967 in parentheses): television sets, 17 (54); washing machines, 6 (33); and refrigerators, 6 (31).

26a. The comparative figures for the Federal Republic (1967) are: 16 per cent; 6 per cent; 2 per cent.

[83]

27. *Statistisches Jahrbuch 1969 der DDR, cited,* p. 457.
28. *Same,* p. 100.
29. *Jugendgesetz der DDR* of May 4, 1964, *Gesetzblatt der DDR,* Part I, No. 4, pp. 75 ff. Cf., for example § 18.
30. Walter Friedrich and Adolf Kossakowski, *Zur Psychologie des Jugendalters* (Berlin: VEB Deutscher Verlag der Wissenschaften, 1962), p. 150.
31. Cf., in addition to footnote 21, Peter C. Ludz, ed., *Studien und Materialien zur Soziologie der DDR* (Cologne-Opladen: Westdeutscher Verlag, 1964), pp. 42, 55 ff., 381–395.
32. Walter Friedrich, *Jugend Heute* (Berlin: VEB Deutscher Verlag der Wissenschaften, 1966), p. 123.
33. *Same,* p. 127.
34. Walter Ulbricht, "Das Programm des Sozialismus und die geschichtliche Aufgabe der SED," *Protokoll der Verhandlungen des VI. Parteitages der SED, 15. bis 21. Januar 1963,* 4 volumes (Berlin: Dietz Verlag, 1963), vol. I, p. 207.
35. Cf. *Die SED,* published by the Bundesministerium für gesamtdeutsche Fragen (Bonner Fachberichte aus der Sowjetzone: n.p., n.d. [1966]), pp. 56–57, and 73; also Richard Herber and Herbert Jung, *Kaderarbeit, cited,* p. 201.
36. According to the CC's official report, published in *Protokoll der Verhandlungen des VII. Parteitages der Sozialistischen Einheitspartei Deutschlands, 17. bis 22. April 1967,* 4 volumes (Berlin: Dietz Verlag, 1967), vol. IV, p. 226.
37. The author has estimated this figure on the basis of various sources from the GDR.
38. *Protokoll der Verhandlungen des VII. Parteitages der SED, cited,* p. 226.
39. The 1950 figures are taken from Carola Stern, *Porträt einer bolschewistischen Partei: Entwicklung, Funktion und Situation der SED* (Cologne: Kiepenheuer & Witsch, 1957), p. 284.
40. Richard Herber and Herbert Jung, *Kaderarbeit, cited,* p. 211. Here the authors are interpreting the Politburo decision of February 17, 1965.
41. *Same,* p. 202.
42. *Same,* pp. 198–207.
43. This paragraph's data about the Central Committee of the SED are taken from the author's book, *Parteielite im Wandel* (Cologne-Opladen: Westdeutscher Verlag, 1970; American edition: Cambridge, Mass.: M.I.T. Press, forthcoming in 1971).
44. Cf. Rensis Likert, *New Patterns of Management* (New York: McGraw-Hill [International Student Edition], 1967), pp. 222 ff.
45. Peter C. Ludz, *Parteielite im Wandel, cited,* p. 43, fn.
46. From the numerous references which could be cited here, cf. for example, Peter Bender, *Zehn Gründe für die Anerkennung der DDR* (Frankfurt am Main: S. Fischer Verlag, 1968).
47. Cf. especially Uwe-Jens Heuer's book, *Demokratie und Recht im neuen ökonomischen System der Planung und Leitung der Volkswirt-*

schaft (Berlin: Staatsverlag der Deutschen Demokratischen Republik, 1965).

48. Cf., for example, Karl A. Mollnau and Werner Wippold, "Kritische Anmerkungen zu einer Schrift über Demokratie und Recht im neuen ökonomischen System," vol. 15, no. 8, *Staat und Recht*, (1966), pp. 1271 ff.
49. *Neues Deutschland*, October 25, 1968.
50. These figures are based on information in the *Statistisches Jahrbuch 1969 der DDR, cited*, pp. 295 ff., and information in L. Albert and W. Riess, "Die aussenwirtschaftlichen Beziehungen zwischen der DDR und der UdSSR," vol. 22, no. 10, *Statistische Praxis*, (1967), pp. 556 ff.
51. *Same*, p. 557.

BIBLIOGRAPHICAL APPENDIX

GENERAL REFERENCES AND
SUGGESTED FURTHER READINGS

Instead of an extensive bibliography, several sources which
are indispensable to the study of developments in the GDR or
easily available for the American reader should be briefly mentioned. In addition, several important new publications both
from and about the GDR, which can be recommended for further
study, will be commented on. More extensive bibliographies can
be found in most of the works listed here. The compiled material
is arranged in accordance with the sequence of chapters in the
present study.

A. GENERAL REFERENCES

  1. Selected East German Sources

    The most important daily newspaper is the party paper,
    Neues Deutschland. Organ des Zentralkomitees der SED
    (25th year, 1970). The weekly paper, *Die Wirtschaft. Zeit-
    schrift für Politik, Wirtschaft und Technik* (25th year,
    1970) and the monthly which is published by the Central
    Committee of the SED, *Einheit. Zeitschrift für Theorie
    und Praxis des Wissenschaftlichen Sozialismus* (25th year,
    1970), are most useful for current economic and political
    orientation.

    Indispensable as reference works on politics and the econ-
    omy are:

    *Handbuch der Volkskammer der Deutschen Demokrat-
    ischen Republik,* published by the Volkskammer of the
    GDR, 2nd election period: Berlin 1957; 3rd election period:
    Berlin 1959; 4th election period: Berlin 1964; 5th election
    period: Berlin 1968.

    Dokumente der Sozialistischen Einheitspartei Deutsch-

[87]

lands. Beschlüsse und Erklärungen . . . , volumes 1–12 (Berlin: Dietz Verlag, 1948–1969).

Statistisches Jahrbuch der Deutschen Demokratischen Republik, published by the Staatliche Zentralverwaltung für Statistik (i.e., the Governmental Central Administration for Statistics), 1st year (1956) to 15th year (1970), (Berlin: Staatsverlag der DDR).

Ökonomisches Lexikon, 2 volumes (Berlin: Verlag Die Wirtschaft, 1967).

For interpretations of the party line and official party resolutions — in addition to the specific *Protokoll der Verhandlungen Des* . . . *Parteitages der Sozialistischen Einheitspartei Deutschlands* (Berlin: Dietz Verlag) — the reader should consult the following works: WALTER ULBRICHT, *Zum Neuen Ökonomischen System der Planung und Leitung* (Berlin: Dietz Verlag, 1966); WALTER ULBRICHT, *Zum Ökonomischen System Des Sozialismus,* 2 volumes (Berlin: Dietz Verlag, 1968–1969).

Official documents indispensable for the evaluation of the period from 1963 to 1970 were published on the occasion of the GDR's 20th anniversary. In the 956 pages of *Das System der Sozialistischen Gesellschafts- und Staatsordnung in der Deutschen Demokratischen Republik. Dokumente,* published by the Deutsche Akademie für Staats- und Rechtswissenschaft "Walter Ulbricht" (Berlin: Staatsverlag der DDR, 1969), the reader will find a reprint of important parts of the 1963 *Programm der Sozialistischen Einheitspartei Deutschlands,* a complete reprint of the 1968 *Verfassung der Deutschen Demokratischen Republik,* and excerpts from several law codes and decrees passed by the Council of State or the Council of Ministers. Some speeches by party or state functionaries on various national and international occasions are also included in this volume.

Finally, to those who are especially interested in the physical geography of the GDR, the following title can be recommended: GERHARD SCHMIDT-RENNER (ed.), *Wirtschaftsterritorium Deutsche Demokratische Republik. Ökonomisch-Geographische Einführung und Über-*

[88]

sicht (Berlin: Verlag Die Wirtschaft, 1959). Although published in 1959, the book is not out of date. It gives an account of the GDR's physical resources, its important industries and industrial regions as well as of its transportation situation. There is also a chapter describing the economic potential of each of the fifteen *Bezirke*.

A comprehensive economic history of the GDR from 1945 to 1967 was published by the Institut für Gesellschaftswissenschaften beim ZK der SED: HANS MÜLLER und KARL REISSIG, *Wirtschaftswunder DDR. Ein Beitrag zur Geschichte der Ökonomischen Politik der SED* (Berlin: Dietz Verlag, 1968). Both books on the economic situation contain numerous tables and charts as well as comprehensive bibliographies.

2. Selected West German Sources

Among the West German publications, the *SBZ-Archiv. Dokumente, Berichte, Kommentare zu Gesamtdeutschen Fragen* (Cologne, semi-monthly, 19th year, 1968), now *Deutschland-Archiv. Zeitschrift für Fragen der DDR und der Deutschlandpolitik* (Cologne, monthly, 3rd year, 1970), offers current analyses of all important events in the GDR. For economic problems one should refer to the *Wochenberichte* of the Deutsches Institut für Wirtschaftsforschung (DIW) (Berlin, 37th year, 1970). The only comprehensive Western reference work, *SBZ von A bis Z. Ein Taschen- und Nachschlagebuch über die Sowjetische Besatzungszone Deutschlands* (1st to 10th editions, Bonn, 1953–1966; 11th edition, 1969) under the new title *A bis Z. Ein Taschen- und Nachschlagebuch über den Anderen Teil Deutschlands*), is published by the Federal Ministry for All-German (now Intra-German) Affairs, as is also the *SBZ Biographie. Ein Biographisches Nachschlagewerk uber die Sowjetische Besatzungszone Deutschlands* (Bonn-Berlin, 1st edition [1961], 3rd edition [1964], 4th edition [in preparation]). While the *A Bis Z* is an alphabetically organized dictionary (of 832 half-size pages) with entries on important topics as well as information on specific terms of the GDR language, the *SBZ Biographie* can be called the East German *Who's*

Who. Both reference books have been improved edition by edition; but they still reflect the political standpoint of their editor, i.e., the Ministry for All-German (or Intra-German) Affairs.

From a critical point of view SIEGFRIED MAMPEL has written on *Die Verfassung der Sowjetischen Besatzungszone Deutschlands. Text und Kommentar*, 2nd edition (Frankfurt am Main & Berlin: Alfred Metzner Verlag, 1966). In this book, which contains a complete reprint of the 1949 Constitution, Mampel comments on each article of the Constitution, contrasting constitutional law with constitutional reality. This work also includes information about the organization and functions of the governmental apparatus (Council of State, Council of Ministers, Ministries). It also has a large bibliography and comprehensive footnotes.

Since the introduction of the "new economic system" in 1963, the SED's policies in the field of education have also become topical for Western observers. The reader, *Zwei Jahrzehnte Bildungspolitik in der Sowjetzone Deutschlands. Dokumente*, edited by SIEGFRIED BASKE and MARTHA ENGELBERT, 2 volumes (Heidelberg: Quelle & Meyer Verlag, 1966), has thus been an indispensable reference book. About 200 texts documenting the development of educational policies from 1945 to 1965 are here reprinted, with a very useful introduction. The two volumes cover general pedagogical problems as well as the various stages of the polytechnical system of education, the regulations for universities and higher learning in general, and the rulings on vocational training.

Finally, for those who are interested in the state of West German scholarship on the GDR, the following article is recommended: PETER LUDZ and JOHANNES KUPPE, "Literatur zum politischen und gesellschaftlichen System der DDR," 10, *Politische Vierteljahresschrift* (1969) 2/3, pp. 328–387. The authors comment on about seventy publications dealing with aspects of East Germany's political development which appeared in West Germany between 1965 and 1969.

3. Recently Published English Monographs

As far as "the other Germany" is concerned, there has been an information lag in the English-speaking world. Since 1968, however, the following serious monographs on the GDR have been published:

DAVID CHILDS, *East Germany* (New York: Frederick A. Praeger, 1969).

JOHN DORNBERG, *The Other Germany* (Garden City: Doubleday, 1968).

JEAN EDWARD SMITH, *Germany Beyond the Wall: People, Politics . . . and Prosperity* (Boston & Toronto: Little, Brown and Co., 1969).

Each of these books contains much helpful information about the GDR, especially for the period starting with the "new economic system" (i.e., since 1963). Among them, Smith's book — though biased in favor of the GDR — contains the most comprehensive presentation of aspects of political, economic, cultural, and social life in East Germany. Like Dornberg and Childs, Smith has traveled frequently in the GDR and has gained a wealth of impressions from these experiences. His analysis is also based on careful research. The book contains a comprehensive bibliography (pp. 307–323) and an English translation of the text of the GDR Constitution of 1968 (pp. 245–272). Smith's general view of the East German political and economic scenery is somewhat different from our own. The same holds for Childs and Dornberg. We have discussed these differences on the occasion of a review article (cf. PETER C. LUDZ, "Discovery and 'Recognition' of East Germany: Recent Literature on the GDR," vol. 2, no. 4, *Comparative Politics* (1969–70), pp. 681–695).

In addition, the systematic and clearly written but short book by ARTHUR M. HANHARDT, *The German Democratic Republic* (Baltimore: The Johns Hopkins Press, 1968) is recommended for an introduction to the political-historical development of the GDR. One of the few per-

[91]

ceptive American experts on the GDR, Hanhardt offers an objective insight into the political, economic, and sociological problems of the country.

B. REFERENCES FOR CHAPTER I: SOME OBSERVATIONS ON SOCIAL AND POLITICAL CHANGE IN THE GDR

No comprehensive presentation of the entire system has yet appeared in the GDR or in the West. Among available West German publications the work of ERNST RICHERT, *Das Zweite Deutschland. Ein Staat, der Nicht Sein Darf* (Gütersloh: Bertelsmann, 1964), is informative, although somewhat out of date, and sympathetic to the GDR. The first attempt at a comprehensive sociological analysis of GDR society was undertaken in the collected volume edited by PETER C. LUDZ, *Studien und Materialien zur Soziologie der DDR* (Cologne & Opladen: West-deutscher Verlag, 1964). In this volume, fourteen authors analyze various areas of GDR society: occupation and family, industry and business, school, university and research, the changes in the ideology, and the emergence of sociology. An extensive bibliography (1,500 titles from 1952 to 1963) supplements the volume, which is, however, somewhat out of date too.

Social and economic structures in East Germany are investigated by DIETRICH STORBECK, *Soziale Strukturen in Mitteldeutschland. Eine Sozialstatistische Bevölkerungsanalyse im Gesamtdeutschen Vergleich* (Berlin: Duncker & Humblot, 1964). This study, completed in 1962, focuses on demographic structures and developments, on the family and on household statistics as well as on occupational, income, and property structures. The investigations are based on statistical data; in many cases, the author quotes comparable figures from West German statistics. Numerous empirical sociological findings are published and commented on in the collected volume edited by the sociologists KURT BRAUNREUTHER and GÜNTHER BOHRING, *Soziologie und Praxis. Beiträge zur Entwicklung der Marxistischen Soziologie* (Berlin: Dietz Verlag, 1965). The emphasis is on sociological

[92]

studies of industry and youth. Consumer behavior in a socialist Germany and horizontal and vertical social mobility patterns are examined. This volume includes articles about Poland, Czechoslovakia, and Bulgaria.

In addition to the volume just mentioned, the study on *Fluktuation. Eine Praxisverbundene, Wissenschaftlich Begründete Betrachtung Über Begriff, Ursachen, Folgen und Eindämmung der Fluktuation im Sozialistischen Industriebetrieb* (Berlin: Verlag Tribüne, 1965) is of interest for those who want to dig deeper into the East German system, especially into the world of labor. This small volume written by GÜNTER BERNARD *et al.*, contains findings from numerous empirical studies on occupational mobility (fluctuation). The reasons for labor fluctuation and individual motivations for occupational changes are listed and discussed. Another work based on empirical material is that by WALTER FRIEDRICH, *Jugend Heute* (Berlin: VEB Deutscher Verlag der Wissenschaften, 1966). Friedrich gives the first concise account of the position of youth in the GDR, their attitudes toward family, marriage, and occupation, as well as toward ideology and politics. As for the problems connected with the socio-economic situation of women in East Germany, the reader may consult the protocol of a conference held by the Deutsche Akademie der Wissenschaften zu Berlin in 1967. Most of the speeches and papers delivered at this conference are published in the volume *Frau und Wissenschaft. Referate und Ausgewählte Beiträge* (Berlin: Akademie-Verlag, 1968). Economic as well as social aspects of women's situation (their education, occupational changes, their family and housekeeping problems, etc.) are treated by various authors.

The minutes of the fourth conference of February 1967 on problems of higher learning, *Die Aufgaben der Universitäten und Hochschulen im Einheitlichen Bildungs-System der Sozialistischen Gesellschaft* (Berlin: Staatsverlag der DDR, 1967) reproduce reports and discussions. This work is indispensable for study of the reorganization of science and research in the GDR.

[93]

The problems of recruiting, of adequate education, and the correct use of the cadres in the party, economic, and governmental apparatuses, which appeared with the introduction of the "new economic system," are discussed in a great number of East German publications. The following may be suggested for further study:

ALFRED LANGE, *Die Ökonomische Weiterbildung von Wirtschaftskadern. Erfahrungen — Probleme* (Berlin: Staatsverlag der DDR, 1965).

RAINER FALKE & HANS MODROW, *Auswahl und Entwicklung von Führungskadern* (Berlin: Staatsverlag der DDR, 1967).

RICHARD HERBER & HERBERT JUNG, *Kaderarbeit im System Sozialistischer Führungstätigkeit* (Berlin: Staatsverlag der DDR, 1968).

C. REFERENCES FOR CHAPTER II: CHANGES IN THE SED (1958–1967) AND THE EMERGING FACTIONS IN THE POLITBURO

The collection of documents, *Selbstzeugnisse des SED-Regimes* (Köln: Verlag Wissenschaft und Politik, 1963), compiled and commented on by ALOIS RIKLIN and KLAUS WESTEN, is most useful for an understanding of the history of the SED. The emphasis is on the analysis of the first Program and the fourth Statute of the SED (both of 1963). The history of the KPD and, since 1946 of the SED, has, in connection with the SED's 20th anniversary, been frequently discussed by East German writers. Out of a long list of publications, the following deserve attention:

20 Jahre Sozialistische Einheitspartei Deutschlands. Beiträge, published by the Parteihochschule "Karl Marx" beim ZK der SED (Berlin: Dietz Verlag, 1966).

Gemeinsam zum Sozialismus. Zur Geschichte der Bündnispolitik der SED, published by the Institut für Gesellschaftswissenschaften beim ZK der SED (Berlin: Dietz Verlag, 1969).

[94]

CAROLA STERN, *Ulbricht. Eine Politische Biographie* (Cologne: Verlag Kiepenheuer & Witsch, 1963; American edition: Praeger, 1965) is a well written biography of Walter Ulbricht, which takes all available material into consideration. At the same time, this book offers the best introduction to the inner party struggles of SED leadership groups through 1963. *Die SED*, a very helpful, systematic, and informative brief study of the history, organization and membership structure of the SED was published (probably in 1967) by the Federal Ministry for All-German Affairs: this small brochure appeared as an issue of the *Bonner Fachberichte aus der Sowjetzone.* PETER CHRISTIAN LUDZ, *Parteielite im Wandel. Funktionsaufbau, Sozialstruktur und Ideologie der Sed-Führung. Eine Empirisch-Systematische Untersuchung* (Cologne & Opladen: Westdeutscher Verlag, 3rd ed., 1970; American edition forthcoming from the M.I.T. Press in 1971) is the first empirical analysis of the leadership groups of the SED from 1958 to 1967. The author examines changes in the organizational system of the SED, in the social composition of the party (especially of the Central Committee and the Politburo) as well as ideological changes. He has focused mainly on the role of the experts, technocrats, and managers, and the possibilities of their influencing the party. In his most recent work, *Die DDR-Elite Oder Unsere Partner von Morgen?* (Reinbek bei Hamburg: Rowohlt Taschenbuch Verlag, 1968), ERNST RICHERT, one of the more sophisticated experts on the GDR, outlines a "psychological" portrait of the members and candidates of the SED Politburo. This small volume contains a wealth of insights.

D. REFERENCES FOR CHAPTER III: WHY IS THERE NO POLITICAL CHANGE IN THE GDR?

ROBERT HAVEMANN, *Dialektik Ohne Dogma? Naturwissenschaft und Weltanschauung* (Reinbek bei Hamburg: Rowohlt Taschenbuch Verlag, 1964): the lectures of the famous scientist present a fascinating new interpretation of dialectical materialism and a critique of the social policies of the SED. Havemann's thinking nevertheless harkens back to the older philosophical revisionism of the twenties and thirties. UWE-JENS HEUER, *Demokratie und Recht im Neuen Ökonomischen System der Planung und Leitung der Volkswirtschaft* (Berlin: Staatsverlag der DDR, 1965) conveys the best insight into critical revisionism in the GDR, which is receptive to Western thought (especially to cybernetics) but is still officially tolerated by the party. In his worthwhile study, *Zehn Thesen für die Anerkennung der DDR* (Frankfurt am Main: S. Fischer Verlag, 1968), PETER BENDER presents all of the arguments from which one could posit a political "liberalization" in the GDR.

E. REFERENCES FOR CHAPTER IV: THE POSITION OF THE GDR IN THE EAST EUROPEAN PACT SYSTEM

Up to now, not many works on the GDR's foreign policy and foreign trade policy have been published in the West. The most up-to-date, although somewhat compressed, general view is given by WALTER OSTEN in his small book, *Die Aussenpolitik der DDR im Spannungsfeld Zwischen Moskau und Bonn* (Opladen: C. W. Leske Verlag, 1969). KONSTANTIN PRITZEL has written a good history of the gradual incorporation of the GDR into COMECON, *Die Wirtschaftsintegration Mitteldeutschlands* (Cologne: Verlag Wissenschaft und Politik, 1969). His investigations are based on official and semi-official materials coming from GDR and Western sources.

NORMAN J. G. POUNDS has produced a penetrating historical and geographical analysis of all of the countries of Eastern Europe in his *Eastern Europe* (Chicago: Aldine Publishing Company, 1969). He conveys excellent insights into the geographical, demographical, and ecological structures of the individual East European countries. In the chapter on the GDR, the description of the economic structure, which is presented in terms of the economy and geography, is especially praiseworthy. The volume contains references to additional specialized literature. A collection of articles, *Wirtschaftsreformen in Osteuropa*, edited by KARL C. THAHLHEIM and HANS-

HERMANN HÖHMANN (Cologne: Verlag Wissenschaft und Politik, 1968), endeavors to demonstrate the connections among economic reforms in the individual East European countries. The volume covers recent economic developments in the Soviet Union, the GDR, Poland, Czechoslovakia, Hungary, Bulgaria, Rumania, and Yugoslavia. In addition, the internationally known experts, ALFRED ZAUBERMAN and GREGORY GROSSMAN, have contributed their more general views to the volume. While Zauberman gives a general evaluation of the models conceived by those who planned the reforms, Grossman balances what has been achieved against structural necessities of communist systems.

From the GDR comes the study *Zur Aussenpolitik der Souveränen Sozialistischen Deutschen Demokratischen Republik* (Berlin: Dietz Verlag, 1967). It is written by PETER FLORIN, one of the leading foreign policy experts in the SED, who is presently GDR ambassador to Prague. His study is concerned with problems of the Warsaw Pact, COMECON, and European security. The book gains value through a chronological table, which includes the important dates of the GDR's foreign policy (1949–1967), and a review of the status of the diplomatic relations of the GDR, which, however, has in the meantime become out of date. The comprehensive official history, *Geschichte der Aussenpolitik der Deutschen Demokratischen Republik. Abriss* (Berlin: Dietz Verlag, 1968), which covers the period from 1949 to 1965, is unique. It is suitable for a quick orientation in the standpoint of the SED on specific questions of foreign policy.

RECENT BOOKS WRITTEN UNDER THE CENTER'S AUSPICES

Development Policy: Theory and Practice, ed. G. F. Papanek, 1968. Harvard University Press. ISBN 0–674–20250–3.

Political Order in Changing Societies, by Samuel P. Huntington, 1968. Yale University Press. ISBN 0–300–00584–4.

Aid, Influence, and Foreign Policy, by Joan M. Nelson, 1968. Macmillan.

International Regionalism, by Joseph S. Nye, Jr., 1968. Little, Brown & Co. 617334.

Turmoil and Transition: Higher Education and Student Politics in India, ed. Philip G. Altbach, 1968. Lalvani Publishing House, Bombay 1.

The TFX Decision: McNamara and the Military, by Robert J. Art, 1968. Little, Brown and Co. 052418.

Korea: The Politics of the Vortex, by Gregory Henderson, 1968. Harvard University Press. ISBN 0–674–50550–6.

The Precarious Republic, by Michael C. Hudson, 1968. Random House. ISBN 0–674–30287.

Political Development in Latin America, by Martin Needler, 1968. Random House. ISBN 0–674–30446.

Revolution and Counterrevolution: Change and Persistence in Social Structures, by Seymour Martin Lipset, 1968. Basic Books. ISBN 0–465–06953–3.

Agrarian Socialism, by S. M. Lipset, revised edition, 1968. Doubleday-Anchor Books.

The Brazilian Capital Goods Industry, 1929–1964, by Nathaniel H. Leff, 1968. Harvard University Press. ISBN 0–674–08090–4.

Economic Policy-Making and Development in Brazil, 1947–1964, by Nathaniel H. Leff, 1968. Wiley.

German Foreign Policy in Transition, by Karl Kaiser, 1968. Oxford University Press. ISBN 0–19–285025–3.

Taxation and Development: Lessons from Colombian Experience, by Richard M. Bird, 1969. Harvard University Press. ISBN 0–674–86840–4.

The Process of Modernization: An Annotated Bibliography on the Sociocultural Aspects of Development, by John Brode, 1969. Harvard University Press. ISBN 0–674–71070–3.

Protest and Power in Black Africa, eds. Robert I. Rotberg and Ali A. Mazrui, 1970. Oxford University Press.

Agricultural Development in India's Districts: The Intensive Agricultural Districts Programme, by Dorris D. Brown, 1970. Harvard University Press. SBN 674–01230–5.

Korean Development: The Interplay of Politics and Economics, by David C. Cole and Princeton N. Lyman, 1970. Harvard University Press. SBN 674–50563–8.

Lord and Peasant in Peru, by F. LaMond Tullis, 1970. Harvard University Press. ISBN 0–674–53914–1.

Peasant Mobilization and Agrarian Reform in Venezuela, by John D. Powell, forthcoming from Harvard University Press. SBN 674–68626–8.

Development Policy II: The Pakistan Experience, eds. Walter P. Falcon and Gustav F. Papanek, forthcoming from Harvard University Press.

Peace in Europe, by Karl E. Birnbaum, 1970. Oxford University Press. ISBN 0–19–2850423.

The Logic of Images in International Relations, by Robert Jervis, 1970. Princeton University Press. 07532–8.

Authoritarian Politics in Modern Society: The Dynamics of Established One-Party Systems, eds. Samuel P. Huntington and Clement H. Moore, 1970. Basic Books. ISBN 465–00569–1.

The Kennedy Round, by John W. Evans. Forthcoming from Harvard University Press. SBN 674–50275–2.

The Politics of Nonviolent Action, by Gene Sharp, forthcoming from The Pilgrim Press.

A Bibliography of Intelligence Activities, compiled and annotated by William R. Harris, forthcoming from Harvard University Press.

Nuclear Diplomacy, by George H. Quester, 1970. The Dunellen Co., Inc.

Peace in Parts? Regional Organizations, Integration, and Conflict, by Joseph S. Nye, 1970. Little, Brown and Co.

The Myth of the Guerrilla, by J. Bowyer Bell, forthcoming from Blond (London) and Knopf (New York).

The Student in Latin America, by Arthur Liebman *et al.*, forthcoming from Harvard University Press.

OCCASIONAL PAPERS IN INTERNATIONAL AFFAIRS

1. *A Plan for Planning: The Need for a Better Method of Assisting Under-developed Countries on Their Economic Policies*, by Gustav F. Papanek, 1961. 12 pp. $.25.
2. *The Flow of Resources from Rich to Poor*, by Alan D. Neale, 1961. 83 pp. $1. ISBN 0–87674–000–X.
3. *Limited War: An Essay on the Development of the Theory and an Annotated Bibliography*, by Morton H. Halperin, 1962. Out of print.
4. *Reflections on the Failure of the First West Indian Federation*, by Hugh W. Springer, 1962. Out of print.
5. *On the Interaction of Opposing Forces under Possible Arms Agreements*, by Glenn A. Kent, 1963. 36 pp. $1. ISBN 0–87674–001–8.
6. *Europe's Northern Cap and the Soviet Union*, by Nils Örvik, 1963. 64 pp. $1. ISBN 0–87674–002–6.
7. *Civil Administration in the Punjab: An Analysis of a State Government in India*, by E. N. Mangat Rai, 1963. 82 pp. $1. ISBN 0–87674–003–2.
8. *On the Appropriate Size of a Development Program*, by Edward S. Mason, 1964. 24 pp. 75 cents. ISBN 0–87674–004–2.
9. *Self-Determination Revisited in the Era of Decolonization*, by Rupert Emerson, 1964. 64 pp. $1.25. ISBN 0–87674–005–0.
10. *The Planning and Execution of Economic Development in Southeast Asia*, by Clair Wilcox, 1965. 27 pp. $1. ISBN 0–87674–006–9.
11. *Pan-Africanism in Action*, by Albert Tevoedjre, 1965. 88 pp. $2. ISBN 0–87674–007–7.
12. *Is China Turning In?* by Morton H. Halperin, 1965. 34 pp. $1. ISBN 0–87674–008–5.
13. *Economic Development in India and Pakistan*, by Edward S. Mason, 1966. Out of print.
14. *The Role of the Military in Recent Turkish Politics*, by Ergun Özbudun, 1966. 54 pp. $1.25. ISBN 0–87674–009–3.
15. *Economic Development and Individual Change: A Social-Psychological Study of the Comilla Experiment in Pakistan*, by Howard Schuman, 1967. Out of print.
16. *A Select Bibliography on Students, Politics, and Higher Education*, by Philip G. Altbach, 1967. 54 pp. $2.50. ISBN 0–87674–011–5.
17. *Europe's Political Puzzle: A Study of the Fouchet Negotiations and the 1963 Veto*, by Alessandro Silj, 1967. 178 pp. $2.50. ISBN 0–87674–012–3.
18. *The Cap and the Straits: Problems of Nordic Security*, by Jan Klenberg, 1968. 19 pp. $1. ISBN 0–87674–013–1.